Women
of the
Grange

**Recent Titles in
Contributions in Women's Studies**

Education for Equality: Women's Rights Periodicals and Women's Higher Education, 1849–1920
Patricia Smith Butcher

Women Changing Work
Patricia W. Lunneborg

From the Hearth to the Open Road: A Feminist Study of Aging in Contemporary Literature
Barbara Frey Waxman

Women, Equality, and the French Revolution
Candice E. Proctor

Serious Daring from Within: Female Narrative Strategies in Eudora Welty's Novels
Franziska Gygax

Verging on the Abyss: The Social Fiction of Kate Chopin and Edith Wharton
Mary E. Papke

The Feminization of Poverty: Only in America?
Gertrude Schaffner Goldberg and Eleanor Kremen, editors

The Dominion of Women: The Personal and the Political in Canadian Women's Literature
Wayne Fraser

Successful Career Women: Their Professional and Personal Characteristics
Cecilia Ann Northcutt

The Life of Margaret Fuller: A Revised, Second Edition
Madeleine Stern

The Sea of Becoming: Approaches to the Fiction of Esther Tusquets
Mary S. Vásquez, editor

Gender Differences: Their Impact on Public Policy
Mary Lou Kendrigan, editor

The World of George Sand
Natalie Datlof, Jeanne Fuchs, and David A. Powell, editors

WOMEN OF THE GRANGE

Mutuality and Sisterhood in Rural America, 1866–1920

DONALD B. MARTI

Contributions in Women's Studies, Number 124

GREENWOOD PRESS

New York • Westport, Connecticut • London

Library of Congress Cataloging-in-Publication Data

Marti, Donald B.
   Women of the Grange : mutuality and sisterhood in rural America,
1866–1920 / Donald B. Marti.
      p.   cm.—(Contributions in women's studies, ISSN 0147-104X ;
no. 124)
   Includes bibliographical references and index.
   ISBN 0–313–25723–X (alk. paper)
   1. National Grange—History.   2. Rural women—United States—
History.   3. Women in agriculture—United States—History.
4. Women farmers—United States—History.   5. Farmers' wives—United
States—History.   I. Title.   II. Series.
HD1485.N39M37   1991
338.1'06'073—dc20   91–11328

British Library Cataloguing in Publication Data is available.

Library of Congress Catalog Card Number: 91–11328
ISBN: 0–313–25723–X
ISSN: 0147–104X

First published in 1991

Greenwood Press, 88 Post Road West, Westport, CT   06881
An imprint of Greenwood Publishing Group, Inc.

Printed in the United States of America

The paper used in this book complies with the
Permanent Paper Standard issued by the National
Information Standards Organization (Z39.48–1984).

10 9 8 7 6 5 4 3 2 1

Copyright Acknowledgment

The author and publisher gratefully acknowledge permission to quote
from *California Golden Inspirations* (California State Grange, 1960).

Contents

Acknowledgments

Several Grangers helped with this study. C. Jerome Davis, who has been a prominent Grange leader and a student of the Order's history for many years, has been an informative and encouraging correspondent. Jeanne Davies, Master of the Colorado State Grange and the first woman to serve on the National Grange Executive Committee, sent me an illuminating letter and some newspaper reports about her Grange career. Dave Howard, historian of the National Grange, read my manuscript and offered suggestions and encouraging comments. Charles Wismer, Master of the Pennsylvania State Grange, made a collection of Grange publications available at his office and offered some helpful suggestions. Judy Massabny, Information Director of the National Grange, answered questions and allowed me to study various materials at the National Grange headquarters. Harry Massey, Director of Membership Development for the National Grange, also answered some of my questions. Finally, Jacqueline Bishop, an active Michigan Granger and formerly director of the computing center at Indiana University's South Bend campus (IUSB), checked various facts and made some instructive observations about recent Grange history.

Many librarians have also helped by copying, lending, and otherwise making materials available. The Note on Sources at the end of this study identifies some of their institutions. I am particularly indebted to Donna Harlan, a friend and librarian here at IUSB.

Other colleagues, mostly at IUSB, have also helped in various ways. Patricia McNeal, an historian and formerly director of our Women's Studies program, let me offer one of her faculty seminars and speak to her classes on the history of American women. Our honors seminar at

IUSB and the history department at St. Mary's College offered similarly valuable opportunities, thanks to Roy Schreiber, our honors director, and Charles Poinsatte of the St. Mary's history department. Gloria Kaufman of our English department, and director of our Women's Studies program, made some helpful suggestions, as did my colleagues in history, Glenn Chesnut, Patrick Furlong, and Charles Tull. Paul Scherer, then chair of our history department, helped me to get some time for this project. Finally, Nancy Grey Osterud of San Jose State University sent valuable suggestions about current scholarship on the history of rural women.

Introduction

The Order of Patrons of Husbandry, more familiarly known as the Grange, has always been a family organization. It has never divided men and women into separate orders, as other secret societies have usually done; that practice reflects the agricultural part of its heritage. Men and women farmers have regularly crossed the boundary separating their spheres to share work and social enjoyments; recent studies by Nancy Grey Osterud, Deborah Fink, and Mary Neth all make that common point. Participating in the Grange with their men, women have always played important, though often formally subordinate, roles in the Order's work. A few women hold high-sounding titles in the Grange now; a great many of their predecessors helped to build and sustain the organization.[1]

Part of the rural world of "mutuality" between men and women that Osterud, Fink, and Neth describe, the Grange has also created opportunities for the sociability and cooperation among women that are other important parts of country life.[2] Grange sisters have worked together to decorate their halls and to prepare food and programs for the Order's meetings. Moreover, their contributions to programs and the activities of the specialized women's committees that first appeared in the 1880s have reflected their shared interests in domestic crafts, child-rearing, and the moral betterment of their communities. Until the nineteenth amendment was added to the United States Constitution, many women also used Grange platforms and publications to demand the vote.

In their special attention to equal suffrage and other public issues of special interest to women, Grange sisters participated in the woman movement that preceded twentieth-century feminism. According to

Nancy Cott's recent study of feminism, men and women have shared that ideology, but the preceding woman movement was exclusively female. Grange women's participation in the movement, therefore, was an expression of sisterhood, one of the exceptions to their relations of mutuality with men.[3]

The suggestion that Grangers were part of the woman movement is hardly original. Douglas Charles Hebb's 1952 M.A. thesis amply describes "The Woman Movement in the California State Grange."[4] But Hebb's discoveries have been so generally ignored that few students of the Grange or of the movement see any connection between their subjects. For example, a kindly scholar, recommended a few years ago as a guide to Grange sources in a midwestern state, opined that investigation of women Grangers' special interests and activities would yield nothing of real interest. And historians of the woman movement, though sometimes a little more encouraging, have shown scant interest in the Grange. Until very recently, they showed little interest in rural life generally. In 1899, Susan B. Anthony praised the Grange for teaching women to regard themselves as equal to men and for supporting the equal suffrage movement, but her flattering words, no doubt calculated to win Grange support for her cause, now impress few scholars.[5] Taking Anthony's words seriously, though not uncritically, this study will ask what Grangers said and did to convince her and other admirers that they deserved extravagant praise, or at least had a potential that flattery might coax into fruition.

Answering that question requires some preliminary description of the Order. As particularly retentive survivors of United States history survey courses may recall, the Grange is a secret fraternal organization that first appeared in 1867, flourished mightily during the 1873 depression, declined abruptly after 1875, and slowly revived starting in the 1880s. Most of its early members were midwestern, but the "second granger movement" that began in the 1880s was predominantly eastern. Despite their different regional strengths, their best general historian argues, the original and second Granges had very much the same purposes. They fostered cooperative enterprises, called for economic reforms, and tried to improve farmers' social and intellectual lives by bringing neighbors together for what were intended to be enjoyable and stimulating meetings.[6]

The Order has always meant to serve farmers in particular, but it has never been an organization of farmers exclusively. The extent of its heterogeneity is illustrated by a 1984 study of the Pennsylvania State Grange, which reports that the members who responded to a questionnaire included 77 farmers; 115 homemakers, some of whom must have been farm women; 28 people in businesses related to agriculture; 200 people who had no vocational connection with farming; 10 students;

and 207 retired people, some of whom must have been retired farmers. A large majority of the members lived in rural areas, just over a quarter lived in small towns, and 8 percent lived in cities. The Pennsylvania Grangers were predominantly rural, but not all were agricultural.[7] The variety of their occupations was similar to that reported for New Hampshire State Grange members in 1912. A state department of agriculture study then estimated that 18,000 of 30,000 New Hampshire Grangers were either farmers or retired farmers; 6,000 were "from the professional, mercantile, and manufacturing classes"; and the rest were teachers, students, and laborers.[8] At about the same time, a woman who had been a Lecturer in a Pennsylvania Grange recalled the challenge of preparing programs for a membership that included "physicians, gentleman farmers, dairymen, motormen, conductors, truckers, fire insurance agent, music teacher, school teachers, housewives, telephone operators, and high school students."[9]

The Order's diversity began with its earliest members. Traditionally, Grangers have recognized Oliver Hudson Kelley and six other men as its founders, but the 1892 National Grange, with prodding from women members, added that Caroline Hall, Kelley's niece and collaborator, was "equal to a founder." Some Grange writers later argued for her recognition as a true founder, but a critical historian objects that those men were "advocates of women's rights" and, therefore, biased. He adds, reasonably enough, that the list of founders is "arbitrary and somewhat implausible" anyhow.[10]

Of all the founders, only Oliver Kelly devoted much of his life to farming. He grew up in Boston, lived in Chicago and Peoria, and then acquired a Minnesota farm in 1849. After fifteen years, he left for Washington and the United States Department of Agriculture. His wife, Temperance Lane Baldwin Kelley, managed the farm during Kelley's absence.[11] The other founders had less agricultural experience. Some grew up on farms, one owned a farm that he bought with his banking and brokerage profits, another was a gardener who became a learned horticulturist and landscape architect, two were clergymen of the Episcopalian and Universalist denominations, and five were federal government employees.[12] Finally, Caroline Hall, the near-founder, was a Bostonian who taught briefly, as did many later Grange women, after she moved to Minnesota. Eva S. McDowell, widow of a founder and herself Treasurer of the National Grange for twenty-six years, guessed that Hall was touched by the "loneliness and isolation of the lives led by the wives of the farmers." However that may have been, Hall was deeply enthusiastic about the Grange and became Kelley's secretary. She did much of the Order's routine organizational work, compiled a songbook, contributed money, and served in the Order's special women's offices. Hall much outlived her interest in the Grange. She spent her last years in Minneapolis, and when she died in 1918, a local news-paper said nothing about her Grange connection. Hall was important then, according to her obituary, because she had left $100,000 to various benevolences around the city.[13]

The earliest Grangers out beyond the circle of founders were not all farmers either. Fredonia Grange, in Chautauqua County, New York, has been called the "First Farmers' Grange in the World" to distinguish it from the Washington, D.C., group that formed Potomac Grange, but its first Lecturer later remembered being embarrassed by his ignorance of agriculture. He accepted his office, which made him responsible for conducting educational programs, because the other members were "mostly village people, who cared no more about farming than I did." At one early meeting, the Lecturer asked the Master why he had omitted the ritual question about the condition of stock and crops, and the Master replied that few members had either. The Lecturer then reported that his own half-dozen chickens were well.[14]

The Order's first constitution apparently excluded such people. Writ-ten in 1868 by the Washington group, it limited membership to people "engaged in Agricultural pursuits."[15] The restriction was not enforced because some leaders, certainly Kelley, doubted its wisdom. Early in 1869, when the members of North Star Grange in St. Paul asked Kelley if they could admit city people, Kelley replied that everyone who loved the country should be welcomed. He observed that people whose work forced them to live in cities often longed for country retreats, and he thought that the Grange should encourage them. He added that "ladies in the cities" were especially suitable Grangers because they "love flow-ers and summer visits to their rural friends."[16]

Recognizing that restriction of membership to people "engaged in Agricultural pursuits" was inconsistent with actual practice, the National Grange relaxed that standard in the 1873 and 1874 revisions of its con-stitution. They simply required that members be "interested in agricul-tural pursuits"; presumably all current members, surely the Fredonia poultry rancher and city women who loved flowers, fit under some more-or-less plausible interpretation of that rule. The standard tightened again in 1875. That year's revision of the constitution not only demanded that members be "engaged in agricultural pursuits," but also that they have no "interest in conflict with our purposes." Then the Grange meant to become a real farm organization.[17]

That was necessary, leaders thought, because in the course of its spectacular growth, the Order had taken in too many completely un-suitable people. Dudley W. Adams, a successful Iowa farmer who was Master of the National Grange from 1873 through 1875, complained in 1874 that the Order was overrun with "speculators, demagogues, small politicians, grain-buyers, cotton-factors, and lawyers."[18] The Order sought a new agricultural purity just as its membership began to drop from 858,050 in 1875 to 124,420 in 1880. When a local Grange Master in Wisconsin asked the Executive Committee of his state Grange whether a rural minister met the tough new standard, he was told that "engaged in agricultural pursuits" meant just what it said. The Order was for men and women who farmed, and for them only.[19]

That changed quickly. Within a few years, the shrinking Order determined that rural ministers and teachers were sufficiently "engaged" in agriculture to qualify for membership. So were people who owned farms but did not work on them, "provided that they are not engaged in land speculation, grain buying, or mercantile pursuits."[20] Such interpretations, and the rule that each local or subordinate Grange was judge of its own members' qualifications, preserved the Order's vocational diversity and extended it to local, or subordinate, units that had restricted membership to farmers when they began. For example, Minnehaha Grange No. 398 in Minnesota started in 1873 with twenty-one farmers but soon admitted the town miller and other respected people. Similarly, Centre Grange No. 11 in Delaware began in 1874 with fifteen farmers, but other sorts of people "were later accepted until nearly all of the influential families of the neighborhood had at least one member who had joined the Order."[21]

Grangers who actively "engaged in agriculture" were hardly representative of the whole farm population.[22] For example, the southerners among them included few plantation owners or tenants; a study of Mississippi Grangers reports that they were far more common in the hill country than in the Delta, that they were mostly small landowners, and that they were all white.[23] Ethnic exclusivity limited Grange membership in other parts of the country as well. A California leader, Ezra Carr, urged Grangers to welcome Scandinavians, while others tried to recruit Germans, but few members of those groups actually joined. In 1940, the historian of Washington State Granges reported a recent increase in Scandinavian and German participation, but she also noted the "universal 'Englishness' " of Grange names before that time.[24] Moreover, an authoritative history of Pennsylvania agriculture and rural society reports that the Grange has generally been strongest in the state's northern counties and weakest in the southeast "because most Pennsylvania German farmers look with disfavor on secret societies of any kind."[25]

Like other Anglo-Saxon Americans, Grangers admired their own ethnic group and distrusted outsiders, particularly immigrants who belonged to suspect churches. In 1892, for example, a Pennsylvania sister told an audience at an important regional gathering that public education "is especially needed at present when a Pope in a foreign country sends his mandate to his subjects" in America.[26] Such rhetoric occurred frequently enough to suggest that Grangers were content with their Protestant, Anglo-American character. Certainly the Minnesotan who explained in 1883 that his subordinate Grange was declining because "Scandinavians are buying out the American farmers and taking away the material for building up the Grange" took the Order's ethnic character for granted.[27]

Catholic and Lutheran leaders were content to let the Order go its way without recruits from their flocks. The Grange was a secret society; Catholic distrust of such organizations led to a firm Vatican condemnation of them in 1894. Similarly, most Lutheran authorities required clergymen to avoid such connections, and some especially strict Lutheran bodies, such as the Swedish Augustana Synod, forbade membership in secret societies to all communicants. Religion also excluded some conservative evangelicals. The National Christian Association called the Grange a disguised Masonic order and the "last hope of the devil."[28]

Ethnicity and church discipline helped to draw the boundaries of Grange membership, as did the Order's self-consciously "modern" spirit, its energetic optimism. "Modern" people, as they have been characterized in recent social historiography, think that hard work, self-denial, and education can make life better in the future than it has been in the past and that society can be reformed; "traditional" folk, on the other hand, expect that the future will be much like the past.[29] The Grange has always stood for modernization by fostering personal and social improvement through study, economic cooperation, temperance, and enlightened treatment of women. A scholar who puts that a little differently calls Grange leaders "Progressives on the Land" who took pride in attracting the "most intelligent and progressive farmers to the Order." Similarly, an enthusiast claimed in 1904 that the "Grange was an exclusive organization by its very nature" though any farmer could join. Many were called, but only progressive farmers chose to answer.[30]

Proud Grangers have always claimed to be progressive, uniquely so in their inclusion of women and frequent promises to improve women's conditions and status.[31] But the Order invites comparison, in those specific terms, with some contemporary organizations, including the Farmers' Alliances, which appeared soon after the Grange enjoyed its first great wave of popularity. The Alliances and the Grange have very different historical reputations; more political than the Grange usually chose to be, the Alliances created the People's Party and, some admiring historians contend, a precious radical tradition. A revisionist study of the early Grange cogently argues that Kelley and some of his associates, particularly in Minnesota, were radical too and that they "developed a movement culture" just as the Alliances did.[32] In any case, whatever their political and ideological similarities and differences, the two movements assigned very much the same roles to women. A recent dissertation about Alliances in Colorado, Kansas, and Nebraska supports that point with observations that closely parallel what this study will show about women in the Grange. Those western state Alliances and the Grange both claimed that women's participation gave them "respectability"; both provided forums in which women voiced their support of prohibition and equal suffrage and inveighed against the drudgery that they thought ruined farm women's physical and mental health; both had prominent and highly articulate women leaders; and both claimed that their meetings provided relief from the isolation that supposedly made farm life stultifying.[33]

Similarly, an essay about North Carolina Alliance women reports that they found opportunities for "public self-expression" in their movement but that those opportunities were "limited by resistance from men within the movement and from other women outside of it." Grange women also found opportunities for self-expression, and some early resistance, in their Order. Moreover, the North Carolina study notes that the Grange "made clear distinctions between most of the offices and ranks women and men could hold," and then goes on to report "no indication that women were ever elected to the office of president of local alliances." North Carolina Alliance women served mostly as secretaries, treasurers, assistant lecturers, and lecturers, which were much the same offices that Grange women, throughout the country, were most likely to fill.[34]

Finally, an essay about midwestern farm organizations makes direct comparisons between women's roles in the Grange and in the Alliances. Both northern and southern Alliances operated in the midwest; the former accepted women members only half-heartedly, excluded them from offices, and gave them fewer opportunities to participate in programs than did the Grange. But the latter was far more encouraging to midwestern women, some of whom became notable leaders in the organization, than either the northern Alliance or the Grange chose to be.[35] The Colorado, Kansas, and Nebraska study also notes a wide variance in Alliance practice. Nebraska and Colorado produced few women Alliance leaders, but several Kansas women achieved local, state, and even national prominence. One of the Kansans, Mary Elizabeth Clyens Lease, became an especially famous campaigner for the People's Party.[36]

Grange women fought no party battles, but some of them took conspicuous parts in the prohibition and equal suffrage campaigns, which also engaged some Alliance women. Grangers such as Eliza Gifford of New York and Jennie Buell of Michigan were as outspoken in those causes as were their Populist counterparts. One of the Grangers' arguments for equal suffrage was the commonplace "home protection" formula, the claim that women needed votes in order to guard their domestic sphere from the larger society's corruption; Alliance and Populist women, who are reported to have "incorporated the ideology of domesticity into the larger goals of Populism," made the same argument. Finally, leaders among Grange and Alliance women shared some very general social characteristics. They were nearly all Protestants, high school graduates, and middle class. Relatively fortunate, they shared a persistent concern about the drudgery and isolation that afflicted too many other farm women.[37]

Grange women also resembled their contemporaries in the Woman's Christian Temperance Union (WCTU) and women's clubs. The clubs, the WCTU, and the Grange began within a few years of each other. The Grange dates its origin from 1867; New England and New York women founded Sorosis and the New England Woman's Club, which were the beginnings of the club movement, in 1868; the WCTU began in 1874. The three groups also inhabited the same cultural neighborhood. Grange women often belonged to the WCTU, venerated Frances Willard, and used her "home protection" argument in their advocacy of equal suffrage. Some of them also joined, or at least admired, the clubs. For example, Kate Hill, who was Lecturer of the California State Grange in 1915, had been President of the California Federation of Women's Clubs a few years earlier.[38] And Mary Mayo, a prominent Michigan Granger, expressed her admiration of the clubs when she met Lucinda Hinsdale Stone, a famous club leader, on a train in the early 1880s. After summoning her courage to approach Stone, she observed that "the Grange was to the country woman what the club was to the city woman, and more; that in the Grange woman stood on an equal footing with man."[39]

Mayo's comparison was apt, although she simplified and exaggerated the practice of equality in the Grange. One clear similarity between the Grange and the clubs was that both encouraged women to exert their domestic influence beyond their individual homes. Founders of the New England Woman's Club saw it as a "larger home" in which women's domestic virtues could extend their range, and Flora Kimball, a famous California Granger, said that the Grange was "but a larger home" that helped women to see that "the word home has a broader significance than the four walls" of their own dwellings.[40] With that justification, both the clubs and the Grange encouraged women to speak and write about a broad range of subjects. The clubs did that more universally than did Granges; Olive Grange No. 189 in eastern Indiana, kept women in the background while the brothers chewed tobacco and talked about crops.[41]

The Grange differed from the clubs and the WCTU and resembled the Alliances in an obvious and absolutely fundamental respect. The clubs and the WCTU were mainly town and city organizations, while the Grange and the Alliances were rural and, in great part, agricultural. That social difference was important to women. Middle-class urban culture, beginning in the late eighteenth century New England, prescribed a sharp distinction between women's and men's "spheres." Barbara Epstein suggests that urban women responded to that segregation by building strong relations with each other. Their temperance movement, which is the manifestation of their solidarity that most interests Epstein, was "shaped by commitment to what were perceived as the interests of women and by antagonism to what was seen as masculine culture."[42]

Rural people also distinguished between women's and men's spheres; though it originated among townfolk, the doctrine of separate spheres had become "hegemonic in American culture by the middle of the 19th century," Nancy Grey Osterud observes.[43] But the line that divided women's and men's spheres was drawn less sharply and crossed more regularly in the country than it was in towns. Osterud reports that women in one New York State farm community "were assigned to a subordinate position within their families" but also shared work and social activities with men. Rather than trying to win respect and power by combining with other women in some exclusive way, they sought to enlarge "the dimensions of sharing in their relations with men" by pursuing "strategies of mutuality." Mary Neth's studies of women in twentieth-century midwestern farm communities and Deborah Fink's investigation of an Iowa community point toward the same conclusion.[44]

The Grange was an expression of and vehicle for mutuality, an organization in which family members worked together. With that in mind, an early Southern Granger assured prospective members that the Order was safe from the "woman's rights" subversion that festered in exclusively women's organizations.[45] But Grange women developed forms of solidarity, or sisterhood, among themselves even as they pursued mutuality with men. They used their opportunities to speak and write in the Grange to address women's problems and to claim, as did their sisters in the clubs and the WCTU, the status of morally and culturally accomplished women, of ladies. An historian of women's clubs suggests that their members were ambivalent about being ladies; they certainly did not repudiate that status, but they resented the limitations that it imposed on them.[46] Grangers showed little of that ambivalence. As rural women and often hardworking farmers, uncertain that they were acknowledged to be ladies, they forcefully asserted their gentility and tried to help other rural women develop ladylike graces.

Grange women's efforts to improve their rural sisters' lives inspired some hopeful expressions of respect. Susan B. Anthony, for example, told the 1899 convention of her National American Woman Suffrage Association that she had always been able to tell a "Granger woman as far off as I could see her, because of her air of feeling herself as good as a man."[47] Similarly, Eliza Gifford, who helped to lead the New York State Woman Suffrage Association, the WCTU, and the Grange, claimed that the last was the "greatest equality club the world has ever known."[48] Anthony and Gifford wanted Grange support for their suffrage movement; perhaps they thought that hyperbole would help to win it. They surely exaggerated Grange women's achievements and the Order's enlightenment. But they had a serious point, which the following chapters will try to explain rather more modestly.

Understanding what the Grange has meant to women must begin with recognition that their equality in the Order, which its official rhetoric has always strongly asserted, acquired more practical significance in subsequent years than it had when the Grange began. Though Grangers never excluded women from membership in local units, nor shunted them into an auxiliary Order, they initially barred the sisters from units above the local, or subordinate, level and confined them to ornamental roles in local meetings. Within a few years, women gained membership in state and national Granges, usually by virtue of their husbands' positions in the Order, and began to participate actively in Grange programs. Then, starting in the 1880s, some women found new opportunities for activity and leadership in specialized women's committees. Their share of Grange offices also increased, especially beginning in the 1890s. Few women became Masters, who head Granges. But many became Lecturers, who conduct Grange programs.

This study traces those developments, generalizes about the kinds of women who exercised leadership in the Grange, and describes a few especially important careers. More of it focuses on the uses that women made of their opportunities to speak at Grange meetings and write for the Order's publications. They mainly wrote and spoke about women's domestic responsibilities, suggesting ways in which farm women could escape drudgery and better serve their families' moral and cultural needs. But some of them also used Grange forums to say that women should vote. Overcoming Grangers' initially cautious, sometimes hostile, view of the equal suffrage movement, they persuaded the Order to pass a long series of resolutions endorsing the reform. The precocious California State Grange came around first, in 1878; a succession of other state Granges fell into line over the next few years. The National Grange endorsed equal suffrage in 1885 but then backed away from the cause until 1893. Though it favored votes for women consistently after that, its 1914 session rejected a resolution that would have called for an equal suffrage amendment to the United States Constitution. A similar resolution passed one year later. Those resolutions and their dates are really incidental parts of the story. Its core is the case that Grange women made for equal suffrage and the debates in which they engaged more conservative fellow Grangers. The record of those debates, which is amply preserved in Grange periodicals and proceedings, shows that a usually reliable historian erred in writing that the Order "never wavered on the question of extending suffrage and equal rights to the fairer sex."[49] The Order's support for women's rights had to be won.

Grangers finally reached a considerable degree of unity in favor of equal suffrage, but their ideology about women retained another, more generalized kind of dissonance. On one hand, vocal women urged their sisters to aspire beyond domesticity, to seek power as leaders of voluntary organizations, including the Grange, and through voting. On the other hand, many of the same women, sisters who took little or no interest in suffrage, and a few brothers who joined the discussion, urged women to beautify their houses, create edifying moral environments for their families, study home economics, and generally try to be ladies. Their advice pointed in two distinct directions, but Grangers usually seemed to think that it was perfectly consistent. Domesticity, they often said, required women to act on the world beyond their home. They knew about Frances Willard's ingenious doctrine of "home protection" and John Ruskin's similar dictum that "woman has a personal work and duty relating to her home, and a public work and duty which is also the expansion of that."[50]

Grangers fully understood the conventional ways of reconciling domesticity and women's claim to public responsibility. But those ideas remained distinct. Grangers wrote and spoke about their synthesis but also about the two ideas separately. Without attempting to count their words, it is reasonable to observe that they said considerably more about domesticity than they did about public responsibility or home protection. The same emphasis guided the sisters' specialized committees. Grangers believed that farm women needed to hear about domesticity because too many of them were failing to create beautiful, gracious, morally edifying homes.

They failed, Grangers routinely argued, because they were overworked. Drudgery kept them ignorant and graceless; it was also thought to drive many of them mad. Grangers depicted overworked farm women who resembled, at their most pathetic, Hamlin Garland's fictional "Lucretia Burns," who was "distorted with work and child-bearing" and "worn as one of the boulders that lay beside the pasture fence near where she sat milking a large white cow." That cow, querulous children, a brutish husband, cooking, and housework drove Lucretia Burns to the edge of madness. She withdrew from her family and refused to work until a young school teacher, concerned about her neglected children, told the suffering woman to "Live and bear with it all for Christ's sake— for your children's sake." Then Lucretia Burns plodded on, "but in what spirit the puzzled girl could not say."[51]

Grangers observed real Lucretia Burnses, but few of the women who wrote and spoke in Grange forums thought that their own predicaments were anywhere nearly that bad. They complained about overwork and male neglect and urged each other to improve their domestic lives, but they did not think of themselves as stultified, demoralized women like Garland's pathetic creation. Grangers, they claimed, were improving; the unprogressive folk who "condemned all things beautiful, and those that have any love for a better life," were unspecified others.[52] Grangers themselves more nearly resembled the teacher. Generally well-educated, often high school graduates, the Grange women who will be described and quoted here had mostly been teachers for at least a few years. They understood the pedagogical role. Sometimes they explained or protested their own problems, but they more generally tried to teach the less fortunate how to live thoughtful, gracious, and satisfying lives.

They also claimed to derive some personal benefits from their activities in the Order. Participating in the Grange gave them opportunities to learn about the techniques of public leadership, especially oratory, and a forum for ideas about everything from pies to equal suffrage. It also made some of them notable figures in their communities, though many of them enjoyed plenty of other opportunities for leadership. Women who played vocal roles in the Grange also participated in their churches, Chautauqua, the WCTU, the Good Templars, and suffrage organizations; a New York Grange woman excused herself from writing very regularly for her state's Grange journal because for "an ordinary farmer's wife to be a member of the Grange, a missionary society, a benevolent society and WCTU (and try to do her part in each) would seem to be enough for her to undertake without writing for a paper."[53] But many women such as Mary Mayo, who was certainly one of the most prominent Grange women in the late nineteenth century, put the Grange first on their short lists of public activities.

They especially valued the Grange because it brought them together with their men, in relationships of mutuality, and also provided occasions for them to work with other women on matters of special concern to their gender. Chautauqua and one of the temperance organizations, the Good Templars, offered the same attraction, but that was exceptional. Women certainly faced a less rewarding situation on Sunday mornings, or so a Pennsylvania Grange sister, who was outraged by a succession of failures to expand women's roles in the Methodist Episcopal Church, complained in 1892. That denomination, then the largest Protestant body in the United States, was arguably the most progressive of the big communions in its treatment of women. But she thought that the Grange took women more seriously than it did, gave them better opportunities for participation and leadership, and deserved more of their energy.[54]

This account of Grange women focuses mainly on the years up to 1920. By that time, they had vastly expanded their first, limited roles in the Order. They had assumed a substantial share of leadership—not parity with male leaders, but dominance of certain offices. They had also persuaded the Order to go on record for equal suffrage and had given each other and their less fortunate sisters a great deal of advice and exhortation about domesticity.

The last chapter, which is really an extended epilogue, takes a general view of the years since 1920, a date that marked a watershed for Grange women, as it did for other organized groups of women. The prohibition and equal suffrage crusades had ended; no new public causes ever commanded so much of their devotion. But, as Nancy Cott argues in *The Grounding of Modern Feminism*, too much emphasis on suffrage can obscure the fact that reform-minded women went on devoting their energies to voluntary organizations after 1920, just as they had done through most of the nineteenth century.[55] Grange women certainly did. They concentrated on the wide variety of civic and private interests that came under the rubric of home economics until the 1980s, when their activities took some new directions and some of them achieved unprecedented stature in the Order. Then, perhaps, mutuality between Grange men and women reached its highest level.

This is intended to be a contribution to the already substantial literature on Grange history. It also provides an opportunity to learn about some rural women and their ideas. Such women have received much less than their due share of historical attention. Scholars have begun to correct that, but historical writing about rural women remains scant.[56] Studying the Grange is one of many possible ways to learn about them.

NOTES

1. Nancy Grey Osterud, " 'She Helped Me Hay It as Good as a Man': Relations among Women and Men in an Agricultural Community" in Carol Groneman and Mary Beth Norton, *"To Toil The Livelong Day": America's Women at Work, 1780–1980* (Ithaca: Cornell University Press, 1987), 87, 91–92; Osterud, "Strategies of Mutuality: Relations Among Women and Men in an Agricultural Community" (Ph.D. diss., Brown University, 1984); Deborah Fink, *Open Country Iowa: Rural Women, Tradition and Change* (Albany: State University of New York Press, 1986), 63; Mary Neth, "Preserving the family farm: Farm families and communities in the Midwest, 1900–1940" (Ph.D. diss., University of Wisconsin, 1987); Neth, "Building the Base: Farm Women, The Rural Community, and Farm Organizations in the Midwest, 1900–1940" in Wava G. Haney and Jane B. Knowles, *Women and Farming: Changing Roles, Changing Structures* (Boulder: Westview Press, 1988), 339.

2. Deborah Fink, *Open Country Iowa*, 77–101 suggests that the intimacy between women that Carroll Smith-Rosenberg describes in her frequently cited "The Female World of Love and Ritual: Relations Between Women in Nineteenth Century America," *Signs* I (Autumn 1975): 1–29 was important to farm women; Jane Marie Pederson, "The Country Visitor: Patterns of Hospitality in Rural

Wisconsin, 1880–1925," *Agricultural History* 58 (July 1984): 355–56 illustrates Fink's point by showing that rural visitors were mostly women, generally preferred to visit female kin, and "tended to act quite independently of the opposite gender." Citing Pederson, Mary Neth argues that "gender networks" were important to rural women and that they shared "work rituals and viewpoints based on gender experience," but that rural sisterhood functioned within neighborhoods that were unified despite gender and other differences. Neth, "Preserving the family farm," 78, note 30. The point for the present purpose is that relations with both men and women were important to members of well-integrated rural communities; the Grange, unlike organizations for women exclusively, fostered both kinds of relationships.

3. Nancy Cott, *The Grounding of Modern Feminism* (New Haven: Yale University Press, 1987), 5.

4. Douglas Charles Hebb, "The Woman Movement in the California State Grange, 1873–1880" (M.A. thesis, University of California, 1950).

5. Susan B. Anthony and Ida Husted Harper, eds., *History of Woman Suffrage* (New York: Arno Press, 1969), 4: 327.

6. Dennis Sven Nordin, *Rich Harvest: A History of the Grange, 1867–1900* (Jackson: University Press of Mississippi, 1974), viii, 42–44.

7. Arba L. Henry, "An Analysis of the Pennsylvania State Grange" (Ed. D. thesis, Pennsylvania State University, 1984), 29.

8. Rexford Booth Sherman, "The Grange in Maine and New Hampshire" (Ph.D. diss., Boston University, 1973), 87–88.

9. *Pennsylvania Grange News* 11 (June 1914): 19.

10. Charles Gardner, *The Grange—Friend of the Farmer* (Washington: National Grange, 1949), 448; William D. Barns, "Oliver Hudson Kelley and the Genesis of the Grange: A Reappraisal," *Agricultural History* 41 (July 1967): 235.

11. Thomas A. Woods, *Knights of the Plow: Oliver H. Kelley and the Origins of the Grange in Republican Ideology* (Ames: Iowa State University Press, 1991), especially chapter 2; Fred Brenckman, *History of the Pennsylvania State Grange* (Harrisburg: Pennsylvania State Grange, 1949), 147 notes that Temperance Kelley let her husband have hundreds of dollars from her legacy for his Grange work in 1868, when he was thoroughly discouraged with the Order's prospects, and made no objection when he mortgaged their home.

12. Gardner, *The Grange*, 436–47.

13. Ibid., 447–48; Eliza Gifford, speech read to the New York State Grange in 1894, in Gifford manuscripts, Patterson Library and Art Gallery, Westfield, New York; *Minneapolis Journal* 26 December 1918; Thomas Clark Atkeson, *Semicentennial History of the Patrons of Husbandry* (New York: Orange Judd Co., 1926), 347–48.

14. Mortimer Whitehead, ed., *A Silver Jubilee: Twenty-Fifth Anniversary of the First Farmers' Grange in the World* (Washington: National Grange, 1893), 9.

15. *Constitution of the Patrons of Husbandry* (Washington: National Grange, 1868), Article V.

16. *The Minnesota Monthly* 1 (April 1869): 120; Kelley seems to have been familiar with the convention of "rural retirement," which had a long history in his native Boston. That convention is best explained in Tamara Plakins Thornton, *Cultivating Gentlemen: The Meaning of Country Life among the Boston Elite, 1785–*

1860 (New Haven: Yale University Press, 1989), particularly 45–50, though the theme runs through much of Thornton's book; Woods, *Knights of the Plow*, 192–93 reports that Kelley organized a subordinate Grange in the borough of Manhattan, New York City.

17. Article V in the 1873, 1874, and 1875 revisions of the Constitution.

18. *Proceedings of the Seventh Session of the National Grange of the Patrons of Husbandry* (New York: National Grange, 1874), 18.

19. *Bulletin* 1 (March 1875); Nordin, *Rich Harvest*, 35–39 considers various reasons, particularly organizational weaknesses, why the Grange lost members so rapidly in the late 1870s.

20. *The Grange. What It Has Accomplished. What It Is Still Laboring to Accomplish. Declaration of Purposes. Who Are Eligible to Membership. And How to Organize a Subordinate Grange.* (Mechanicsburg: Farmer's Friend, 189[?]), 33.

21. Paul Hesterman, "The History of Edina," undated typescript in Minneapolis Public Library, 14–16; Sue S. Carpenter, "History of Centre Grange From 1874 to 1949" in *History of Centre Grange No. 11 Patrons of Husbandry 1874–1974* (Centreville, Delaware: Centre Grange No. 11, 1974), 4.

22. Nordin, *Rich Harvest*, 25, 31–32, says that the Order "represented a cross-sampling of American rural life" and then notes that it excluded blacks and people who were considered immoral. He also comments on the paucity of immigrants in the Grange.

23. Robert Arnold Calvert, "The Southern Grange: The Farmer's Search for Identity in the Gilded Age" (Ph.D. diss., University of Texas, 1969), 42; James S. Ferguson, "The Granger Movement in Mississippi" (M.A. thesis, Louisiana State University, 1949), 56.

24. *Bulletin* 3 (February 1877); Calvert, "The Southern Grange," 52; Harriet Ann Crawford, *The Washington State Grange 1889–1924: A Romance of Democracy* (Portland: Binfords and Mort, Publishers, 1940), 60–61.

25. Stephen Whitcomb Fletcher, *Pennsylvania Agriculture and Country Life, 1840–1940* (Harrisburg: Pennsylvania Historical and Museum Commission, 1955), 413.

26. *Farmer's Friend and Grange Advocate* 19 (10 October 1892): 1.

27. Ms. minutes of the Minnesota State Grange, 18 December 1883, 6, in Division of Archives and Manuscripts, Minnesota Historical Society.

28. Jay Dolan, *The American Catholic Experience* (Garden City: Doubleday and Co., 1985), 313; Henry Eyster Jacobs, *A History of the Evangelical Lutheran Church in the United States* (New York: The Christian Literature Co., 1893), 477–78; Fritiof Ander, "The Immigrant Church and the Patrons of Husbandry," *Agricultural History* 8 (October 1934): 155–68.

29. Richard D. Brown, *Modernization: The Transformation of American Life, 1600–1865* (New York: Hill and Wang, 1976), 10–13; James McPherson, *Ordeal By Fire: The Civil War and Reconstruction* (New York: Alfred A. Knopf, Inc., 1982), 13–21.

30. Sister M. Thomas More Bertels, O.S.F., "The National Grange: Progressives on the Land" (Ph.D. diss., Catholic University of America, 1962), 17, 46.

31. Charles Gardner, the Order's own best historian, says that it "turned on the radiant light of hope for rural women." Gardner, *The Grange: Friend of the Farmer, 1867–1947* (Washington: National Grange, 1949), 191. Dennis Sven Nor-

din, an outside historian who caught the Grange spirit, makes much the same assertion. Nordin, *Rich Harvest*, 193.

32. Lawrence Goodwyn, *Democratic Promise: The Populist Movement in America* (New York: Oxford University Press, 1976); Woods, *Knights of the Plow*, xv–xx disputes Goodwyn's characterization of the Grange as conservative and does for it what Goodwyn does for the Alliances.

33. MaryJo Wagner, "Farms, Families, and Reform: Women in the Farmers' Alliance and Populist Party" (Ph.D. diss., University of Oregon, 1986), 2, 9–10, 18, 148–49.

34. Julie Roy Jeffrey, "Women in the Southern Farmers' Alliance," *Feminist Studies* 3 (Fall 1975): 72–91.

35. Vanette M. Schwartz, "The Role of Rural Women in Midwestern Farm Organizations, 1870–1900," an unpublished paper presented to the "Female Sphere Conference" at New Harmony, Indiana in 1981.

36. Wagner, "Farms, Families, and Reform," v, 19, 52–55, 147.

37. Ibid., v, 19, 147; the Grange side of this comparison will be developed in Chapter 2.

38. *National Grange Monthly* 12 (July 1915): 5.

39. Jennie Buell, *One Woman's Work for Farm Women* (Boston: Whitcomb and Barrows, 1908), 30–32.

40. Karen J. Blair, *The Clubwoman as Feminist: True Womanhood Redefined, 1868–1914* (New York: Holmes and Meier Publishers, Inc., 1980), 32; Flora Kimball, "Woman's Relationship to Society Through the Grange," an undated leaflet from the National Grange Lecture Department with similar leaflets in the National Agricultural Library, also published in the *Husbandman* 14 (11 January 1888): 3.

41. Minutes of Olive Grange No. 189, 1887–1892, in Indiana Historical Society.

42. Barbara Leslie Epstein, *The Politics of Domesticity: Women, Evangelism and Temperance in Nineteenth-Century America* (Middletown: Wesleyan University Press, 1981), 7, 35–36, 125.

43. Osterud, "Strategies of Mutuality," 3.

44. Osterud, " 'She Helped Me Hay It as Good as a Man' ", 87, 91–92; Neth, "Preserving the Family Farm"; Neth, "Building the Base;" Fink, *Open Country Iowa*, 63.

45. William E. Simmons, *How I Came to be a Patron* (N.p.: National Grange, Bryan Fund Publication No. 2, n.d.), originally published in the *Rural Carolina* (December 1871).

46. Blair, *The Clubwoman as Feminist*, 1–4.

47. Anthony and Harper, eds., *History of Woman Suffrage*, 4: 327.

48. Eliza C. Gifford, address to the New York State Grange, Feb. 1894, in Gifford manuscripts, Patterson Library and Art Gallery, Westfield, New York.

49. Nordin, *Rich Harvest*, 193, 35; Marti, "Sisters of the Grange."

50. Ruth Bordin, *Woman and Temperance: The Quest for Power and Liberty, 1873–1900* (Philadelphia: Temple University Press, 1981), 56; *The Husbandman* 18 (24 February, 1892): 2.

51. Hamlin Garland, "Lucretia Burns" in *Other Main-Travelled Roads* (New York: Harper and Brothers, 1910), 81, 115.

52. *Journal of Proceedings of the Thirteenth Annual Session of the Pennsylvania State Grange* (Mechanicsburg: State Grange, 1885), 34–36.

53. *Husbandman* 17 (31 December 1890): 20.

54. *Farmers' Friend and Grange Advocate* 19 (1 October 1892): 1.

55. Cott, *The Grounding of Modern Feminism*, 85.

56. Vivian B. Whitehead, *Women in American Farming: A List of References* (Davis: Agricultural History Center, 1987); Elizabeth Fox-Genovese, "Women in Agriculture during the Nineteenth Century" in Lou Ferleger, ed., *Agriculture and National Development: Views on the Nineteenth Century* (Ames: Iowa State University Press, 1990), 267–301.

1

Graces, Lecturers, and the Changing "Appearance of Equality"

Women were part of the Grange almost from its first stirring in Oliver Hudson Kelley's imagination. Early in 1866, while touring the south making observations for the United States Department of Agriculture and President Andrew Johnson, Kelley noticed in his "intercourse with the planters," who might have been expected to show some hostility to a Massachusetts Yankee lately from Minnesota, that "it was evidently no disadvantage to be a member of the Masonic fraternity, and as such I was cordially received." In fact, Freemasonry was enjoying a great surge of popularity then; membership grew from nearly 194,000 in 1860 to 446,000 ten years later. Observing that, and sharing Andrew Johnson's hope for a swift national reunion, Kelley imagined a "Secret Society of Agriculturists" that would help to "restore kindly feelings" between the sections. He immediately mentioned the idea in a letter to his niece, Caroline Hall, and discussed it with her a little later that spring. She suggested that women be allowed full membership in the new order. Kelley's 1875 history of the Grange recalls, with strong typographical emphasis, that "THIS FEATURE ORIGINATED WITH HER."[1]

Hall's idea was genuinely original. Earlier agricultural societies had limited membership to men, though women had been welcome to participate in their fairs; existing fraternal organizations, other than the Good Templars, either excluded women or confined them to side degrees. Indeed, a historian of Freemasonry suggests that men enjoyed the fraternity in part because it was all male. It got them away from their wives, whom Masonic jokes characterized as "domestic tyrants."[2] Masons, another scholar argues, rejected the orthodox nineteenth-century "identification of women as the moral custodians of society . . .

and claimed that men could attain morality through participation in an all-male brotherhood."[3] In any case, however they understood female authority, Masons clearly valued their lodges as sanctuaries from women's superintending eyes. The Grange would offer no sanctuary.

The idea of a rural fraternity lay fallow for a year after Kelley's discussion with Hall. He began to think about it again soon after taking a frustrating job with the Post Office Department in Washington and then discussed it with William M. Ireland, a fellow Mason and postal worker who would soon be the first Treasurer of the National Grange. Ireland encouraged Kelley to devise rituals for the proposed Order. An early result was a first degree for women that Kelley sent to Caroline Hall for comment.[4] Kelley also consulted with William Saunders, a horticulturist and landscape architect who then worked for the United States Department of Agriculture. Saunders' became the first Master of the National Grange; some witnesses to its early history considered him a more important founder than Kelley.[5] One of Saunders' contributions to the Grange was the interest of his friend Elizabeth Thompson, a wide-ranging reformer and philanthropist whose money paid for some of the new Order's promotional literature. Interested in cooperative agricultural colonies, temperance, equal suffrage, and women's medical training, among other causes, she supported the Grange only briefly but at a critical juncture. In 1879, she helped Saunders, who was then disaffected from the Grange, to start the American Workers' Alliance, which promised to treat men and women as equal members.[6]

Kelley's history emphasizes Anson Bartlett's role in developing a place for women in the Order. Bartlett was an Ohio dairyman and cheesemaker who became the first Overseer of the National Grange. He had written feelingly about women dairy farmers, who were "prematurely wrinkled, decrepit and old" because of their continual drudgery, before he had any contact with Kelley.[7] In September 1867, Kelley told Bartlett that he wanted women to be in "full communion" with the Grange and represent the Roman graces Ceres, Pomona, and Flora in rituals. He said nothing about electing women to offices; the graces, as Kelley thought of them in 1867, were merely ceremonial figures. The 1869 *Manual and Monitor of Subordinate Granges* listed the graces as officers and then prescribed rites for their installations, but it added nothing to their functions. They simply posed fetchingly during Grange meetings and spoke a few lines about grain, fruit, and flowers.[8]

Bartlett pressed Kelley to sustain his commitment to women. In November 1867, for example, Bartlett complained that Kelley's draft constitution required them to pay excessively high membership fees and dues. Rather than paying ten dollars for membership and twenty-five cents in monthly dues, which the draft proposed for all members, Bartlett thought that women should pay less than men because they had less money. Caroline Hall soon made the same point. Women, she guessed, could earn only half of what men got, an injustice that she hoped "this Society will correct." Kelley promptly agreed. He told Bartlett that he had always believed "that if a female does the same work as a man, she is entitled to the same pay he receives." Lacking any immediate way to achieve that reform, the Grange founders agreed on a two-dollar membership fee for women, as opposed to ten dollars for men, and required each local Grange to pay its state unit twenty-five cents for every man and twelve cents for every woman four times a year.[9]

Bartlett sharply criticized Kelley early in February 1868 for having devised only one degree for women. Because men already had four degrees, Bartlett feared that Kelley meant to confine women to an inferior, auxiliary place in the Order. Other fraternal organizations had done that much for women; Bartlett thought that Kelley had meant to take the Grange further. "I am not what is popularly called a 'Woman's Rights man,'" Bartlett told Kelley, but he thought that equality of the sexes was on its way and hoped that the Grange would lead instead of follow. The Order, he added, should have "at least the appearance of equality; varied, of course, to suit the condition of the sexes." Without that appearance, it would repel the "earnest, active, energetic women" who would make useful members. Kelley replied, "I agree with you in every particular." If women would bear with him, briefly, "we will have four ceremonies for them that will eclipse all the rest."[10]

Whether the women's degrees eclipsed the men's is doubtful, but at least until 1889, when the Order published degree ceremonies in which men and women could participate together, women heard ritual language that extolled their special virtues and reminded them of their special responsibilities. They continued to hear such language in many Granges that used older rituals well into the present century. New sisters, for example, were urged to "imitate the *modesty* and usefulness of the humble grass." The initiation also praised ancient mythology, which was an important source of Grange doctrine and ritual, because it "invariably chose the type of woman as superior to man." Finally, the new sister heard that she "was intended by her Creator to be neither the slave, the tyrant, nor the toy of man, but to be his helpmeet, his companion, his equal." And not just equal—in all of the finer qualities of "mind and heart"—she was only a "little lower than the angels" and a great deal higher than her male associates.[11]

The Order adopted another ceremonial tribute to women in 1875. Whoever led the ritual for dedicating Grange halls, either a state Grange Master or someone deputized by him, was instructed to say that the "Grange door swings inward as readily at the gentle knock of woman as to the ruder knock of man." Once admitted, the speech continued, women were to have an "equal voice" and a full share of the Order's "most exalted honors." Not only would the Grange treat women as equals within the Order, but it would also work for their deliverance from subjugation in the world outside. Great civilizations had long honored women in the abstract, the speaker was to say, but they had showed too little consideration for women themselves. Woman's "rights were limited to the capricious concessions of her lord and master." Now that would change because this "noble Order bears her up upon its strong right arm, and holds above her its shield of protection."[12]

Grange women surely heard all of the flattering and chivalrous words that they could possibly have wanted. The question that required some additional thought, and that occasioned a little mild controversy, was exactly what women were supposed to do in the Order. Only one part of their role was clear from the start: they were supposed to elevate the social tone of Grange meetings. Kelley told Bartlett in a September 1867 letter that "our wives and daughters are generally attractive features of rural life," and their presence would "make the meetings of the Lodges sociable reunions." They add "refinement to our meetings," Kelley told another correspondent a few years later.[13] The Reverend Aaron Grosh, a Universalist minister who was the first Chaplain of the National Grange, made the same point at greater length in his 1876 book on Grange doctrine and ritual. He wrote that woman's "gentle influence, her innate tact in all matters of good taste and propriety, her instinctive perception of righteousness and purity" were essential to the Grange.[14]

Grangers repeated Grosh's formula in only slightly varied terms throughout the whole period of this study. Women, they said, made the Grange different from merely masculine organizations. Men could get away with "rough ways, rude and uncouth expressions and low witticisms" in all-male organizations, a Wisconsin Grange woman opined in 1878, but women's influence forced them to do better in the Grange.[15] A Pennsylvania sister later explained that the Grange resembled a good family in which men supplied "rude and vigorous force," while "woman softens the rudeness, tempers the strength, and adds the refinement of her more sympathetic impulses to his energy."[16] Similarly, a male state Grange Lecturer used part of his 1908 report to say that "woman is more refined, naturally, and of purer tastes than man." He thought that was universally recognized.[17] But an article in the *National Grange* magazine, just a year earlier, said that women's refining influence was too little understood even by themselves. Its appreciation and exercise were vitally important in the country, the article went on, because rural men were especially apt to be coarse "unless restrained by woman's gentleness." Centuries of women's care had made Jersey cattle wonderfully genteel animals; with enough persistence, rural women might yet have the same effect on their men folks.[18]

Women's influence was supposed to make the Grange a sort of rural finishing school, but gentility was not as universal as Grange leaders hoped that it might be. In 1889, for example, Olive Grange No. 189 in eastern Indiana, where the sisters kept in the background, and brothers had to be reminded to bring "their women" to an installation of officers, bought six spittoons for its hall. The members probably thought that was enough for a group that would rarely have had more than twelve men present, but two years later, they voted to fine brothers who continued to spit on the floor. Penalties escalated from five cents for the first offense to expulsion for the fourth. The Olive Grangers aspired to gentility, for which women were particularly responsible, but the Order's uplifting influence was working slowly in their part of Indiana.[19]

Women could exert their influence without lifting a hand, by their mere presence and a few disapproving looks, but they did much of the Order's routine work as well. That started with Caroline Hall, Kelley's niece and secretary, who sewed Grange regalia, compiled a songbook, and contributed money at a critical point.[20] Later Grange women followed her industrious example. They cleaned Grange halls, devised entertainments, often planned entire programs, and prepared meals. Cooking, predictably, was a regular part of women's Grange work. Reports of local Grange meetings frequently thanked the sisters for splendid repasts. Fearful that the effort spent in Grange kitchens was limiting women's enjoyment of the Order's social and intellectual opportunities, a New Jersey unit with exceptionally radical leadership simplified its menu to sandwiches, popcorn, fruit, and nuts.[21] But few Granges shared that concern. They cheerfully accepted women's culinary and other efforts to make their meetings gracious and enjoyable. Typically appreciative, New Jersey's State Grange Master observed in 1880 that the strongest local Granges were "those where woman's influence is exerted to make the meetings interesting," and a friendly observer of early California Granges guessed that "one lady is equal to six men and a span of horses."[22] Exerting influence went far beyond feminine restraint of male vulgarity.

As vital as women's presence and labor were acknowledged to be, Grangers hesitated to extend their sisters' participation beyond the local, or subordinate, level. The first National Grange constitution implicitly excluded them from the National and state Granges. Written by the little circle of founders in 1868, the constitution said that state Granges would consist of Masters and Past Masters of subordinate Granges and that Masters and Past Masters of state Granges would comprise the National Grange. Because no women had yet become Masters, and none would be Master of a state Grange for another twenty-five years, women were effectively excluded from the Order's higher units.[23] The first state Grange, organized by Minnesota's ten subordinates in February 1869, departed from the constitution by including secretaries in the absence of Past Masters, but it was an exclusively male gathering,[24] as was the first representative National Grange, which met in Kelley's Georgetown parlor in January 1873, though "four ladies honored the body" by observing its deliberations.[25]

The 1873 National Grange adopted a new constitution, which required that future sessions be composed of "Masters of State Granges and their wives who have taken the degree of Pomona." Women have participated in the National Grange ever since, although one account of the 1874 session says that most of them sat apart from the men, and a sister in the 1878 National Grange took the floor to warn against an effort to exclude women.[26] Similarly, the new constitution said that state Granges would consist of subordinate Masters and their wives, if the wives were Grange members. That proved difficult to apply as subordinate Granges multiplied during the next two years. Iowa had 718 subordinate Granges late in 1872 and 1,999 two years later; proliferation in Missouri and Indiana was only a little less rapid, and other states were just off that pace.[27] State Granges tried to hold their annual meetings down to manageable size by electing delegates from the mass of subordinate Masters. That had the effect of excluding women until an 1876 amendment to the National Grange constitution stipulated that the wives of elected delegates were delegates as well.[28] Women have since been a substantial part of state Grange membership, though most of them have participated by virtue of their husbands' positions.

The Order also passed through some early uncertainty about whether women would hold offices. The first constitution required that every Grange have nine officers: Master, Lecturer, Overseer, Steward, Assistant Steward, Chaplain, Treasurer, Secretary, and Gate Keeper. Women had a tiny share of those posts in the Order's first twenty years. Formal leadership, clearly, was a male prerogative. Within one year of writing that first constitution, however, the Grange acquired four additional officers: Ceres, Pomona, Flora, and Stewardess. The first three, the Roman graces of grain, fruit, and flowers, were part of the Grange ritual that Kelley tested in the Potomac Grange, a sort of rehearsal group that consisted mainly of government clerks, early in 1868. They became officers one year later. The office of Stewardess, which also appeared in 1869, has been called Lady Assistant Steward at least since 1873. Only women can hold those four offices, and therefore, no Grange can meet in due form without at least four women. The first constitution required "nine persons" to start a new Grange, but later revisions assured an adequate supply of women officers by requiring "Nine men and four women."[29]

That new language may have implied that the nine original offices were reserved for men, just as the four additions were reserved for women. No Grange document ever said that explicitly, but the Reverend

Aaron Grosh suggested some such understanding in 1876. He wrote that women were eligible for every post in the Order "except, perhaps, the few offices whose titles and duties would probably render them undesirable to the sex," much as the titles and duties of the women's offices "would be improper and undesirable to men." Grosh probably meant that only men should be Masters, Overseers, and Stewards.[30] The idea that some places were for men exclusively had enough support so that the editor of New York's Grange organ, *The Husbandman*, warned in 1875 that the National Grange might be about to bar women from the most responsible offices; he suggested that Granges anticipate the ruling by electing only men to their top positions.[31] California's state Grange Master tried to resolve the uncertainty in 1873 by ruling that all members were eligible for all of the Order's offices but, despite that clarification, men did not try to become graces and no woman sought real leadership in the California State Grange for another three years. Then Jeanne C. Carr, who went on to become one of the most prominent women Grangers in the state, narrowly failed to be elected Lecturer.[32]

Ceres, Pomona, Flora, and Lady Assistant Steward were the offices with which Grange women began and the offices in which they have always been most likely to serve. Their character is suggested by the rank assigned to them in the 1873 constitution; they were placed, very explicitly, at the bottom of the hierarchy.[33] Perhaps for that reason, Grangers were less likely to vote for those offices than for the others. At the Iowa State Grange meeting of 1875, for example, candidates for Master got a total of 87 votes. Totals for the other offices were: Overseer, 84; Lecturer, 79; Steward, 77; Assistant Steward, 77; Treasurer, 71; Chaplain, 70; Gate Keeper, 70; Flora, 61; Lady Assistant Steward, 58; Ceres, 57; and Pomona, 46.[34] In the same year, Wisconsin State Grange members cast 253 votes for Master and 35 for Pomona, the women's office that drew the most votes.[35] Perhaps male Grangers abstained from voting for the "lady officers"; they sometimes left women's matters entirely to women, as did the 1875 National Grange meeting that appointed a special committee of sisters to consider a resolution on dress reform.[36] If that partly accounts for the small number of votes cast for women officers, it also strengthens the impression that the women's offices were not vitally important to the Order as a whole.

Unlike most of the other officers, the women had purely ceremonial functions. They spoke some ritual words and posed in their ceremonial places. Kelley thought that women enjoyed such activities. Late in 1868, he told Francis McDowell, an early Grange leader who took a particular interest in ceremonies, how pleased women seemed to be with the roles and regalia that he was designing for them. The Grange was a "fancy dress party," he wrote, and women "like that, you know."[37] But some of the women officers found their wholly ornamental roles frustrating.

Mrs. J. B. Olcott, Pomona of the Connecticut State Grange, showed as much in 1887 when she asked why the "three Lady graces sit in distressing dignity, like so many wax-figures, almost" when useful work might be found for them. Having a lively writing style, Olcott thought that the graces might take a hand in Grange "literary work."[38]

Some graces did that. They were auxiliary Lecturers, in effect, and sometimes used their positions to advance ideas about women's education, equal suffrage, home economics, and other matters that concerned them. In 1887, for example, Mary Mayo reported that she had given fifty lectures in various places as Pomona of the Michigan State Grange. She talked about ways in which women could improve their houses, families, and minds.[39] Elizabeth H. Patterson of Maryland, another industrious grace, told readers of the *National Grange* magazine early in this century that every Ceres should "raise aloft the banner of home," which Patterson did by writing articles on home economics, persuading the National Grange to create a home economics committee, and chairing that committee for several years.[40] Similarly, Dr. Hannah McK. Lyons, M.D., Ceres of the Pennsylvania State Grange, wrote about various aspects of hygiene for Grange publications, chaired the state Grange committee on home economics, and helped to raise money for Grange Hall at Pennsylvania State College; Lyons Hall commemorates her services to Penn State.[41] Mayo, Patterson, Lyons, and some other women stretched the limits of their offices, but most of the reports that the "lady officers" submitted to Grange meetings indicate that they found few opportunities to do that. Cordelia Atkeson, for example, told the 1901 National Grange that there was no "real reason" for her report as Ceres because the office had given her nothing to do.[42] Clara L. Williams, Lecturer of the Maryland State Grange, noted the same problem among local graces in or near 1924, when she suggested that they be put in charge of committees in order "to make their offices more worthwhile."[43]

Early Grangers generally expected women to be content with their own special offices, but a scattering of women occupied the typically male offices during the Order's first twenty years. In 1875, a correspondent told New York's Grange journal that he or she knew of two women Masters of subordinate Granges and "many" women Lecturers, Secretaries, and Chaplains. The editor thought that was probably right, though he reported that women in the most recent National Grange, "evidently bound by their sense of propriety, had favored restricting those offices to men."[44] Throwing propriety to the winds, a subordinate Grange in Howard County, Indiana, elected a woman Master in 1877—she asked members to judge her charitably—and Flora Kimball, an outspoken equal suffrage advocate, became Master of her Grange in San Diego County, California, one year later. By that time, California had a few women Overseers and women Lecturers, common a generation later, who were still rare enough to excite comment.[45] At the state level, Julia Garretson broke new ground when she became Lecturer of the Iowa State Grange in 1874. She questioned her ability but comforted her "doubting heart with the assurance that my mission to the sisterhood may strengthen and encourage many." The historian of Iowa's State Grange calls her a "remarkable success," though she complained that the job was hard and inadequately rewarded. She traveled 8,500 miles to give seventy public lectures in 1874 and received only travel expenses for her pains.[46]

The roster of state officers that appeared in National Grange *Proceedings* for almost a century starting in 1879 show a broad pattern of change in women's share of leadership. They listed Masters, Treasurers, and Secretaries for three years and added Lecturers in 1882. The 1879 roster listed officers in thirty-eight states; that later fluctuated between twenty-nine and thirty-six. Never before 1895 was any woman Master of a state Grange, nor did more than seven women hold the listed offices in any one year. In 1895, when Sarah G. Baird began her seventeen years as Master of the Minnesota State Grange, six other women held leading offices in the thirty-five state Granges. Three states, including Minnesota, had women Secretaries; three, again including Minnesota, had women Treasurers; and no state had a woman Lecturer that year, though several states had elected women Lecturers earlier. In no year through 1895 did women hold more than 5 percent of the principal working offices in the state Granges.[47]

Their share increased markedly in the next quarter-century. Two states had women Lecturers in 1896, four a decade later, and thirteen in 1916. Three states had women Secretaries in 1896, seven in 1906, and ten in 1916. Thirty women served in the four principal executive offices of the thirty-three state Granges in 1920. One of that year's leaders, Pearl Stillwell of Wyoming, was a Master. Ten were Lecturers, two were Treasurers, and seventeen were Secretaries. Women increased their proportion of state leadership to about 22 percent, but their share of Masters' chairs did not increase and the number of women Treasurers dropped by one. Two offices, Lecturer and Secretary, accounted for all of the growth.[48]

States varied widely in the proportion of responsible offices that they assigned to women. In general, women got their largest shares of such places in states where the Order was least firmly rooted. Wyoming, Montana, North Dakota, South Dakota, and Oklahoma, all of which organized state Granges relatively late—in this century—reported large proportions of women officers. Wyoming elected a woman Master once, women Lecturers seven times, and women Secretaries eight times between the formation of its state Grange in 1913 and 1920. South Dakota's

State Grange, which organized in 1909, chose women Lecturers for all of the next twelve years.[49]

Among the older state Granges, Minnesota, the oldest of all, elected women to the four offices forty-nine times between 1895 and 1920. Sarah Baird was Master for seventeen years during that period. Michigan elected women thirty-nine times, which included twenty-four Lecturers' terms. Other old state Granges that had more than ordinarily large numbers of women Lecturers, Secretaries, and Treasurers were: Oregon, 34 terms; California, 28; Kentucky, 26; Indiana, 20; and Illinois, 19. Apart from Kentucky, the states that were most receptive to women's leadership were western or midwestern.[50]

The southern states elected few women leaders, but most of their Granges disbanded before other states elected many either. South Carolina, Tennessee, and Texas, the last Confederate states represented in the National Grange, all dropped out after the 1906 session. The south had no state Granges for almost a quarter of a century after that. Other state Granges managed to function through the whole period from 1879 to 1920 without ever electing a woman to any of the four offices. Delaware, Maine, New Hampshire, Vermont, and West Virginia all maintained perfect consistency. And Massachusetts, Connecticut, New York, Pennsylvania, and Ohio rarely elected women officers. Massachusetts chose a woman Lecturer four times; Connecticut chose a woman Lecturer four times and a woman Secretary three times; New York elected a woman Lecturer five times; Ohio elected a woman Secretary four times; and Pennsylvania elected a woman Secretary five times.[51]

The states in which women were most likely to appear in the top offices were generally those in which the Order was weakest. Strong state Granges kept leadership in male hands, though women were certainly welcome to do much of the essential work in subordinate, or local, Granges. Women increased their share of responsible offices at that level far more impressively and uniformly than they did in the state Granges. For example, Pennsylvania, a state that elected few women to important state offices, developed a very different pattern at the local level. In 1894, its 572 subordinate Granges had three women Masters, 145 women Secretaries, and 121 women Lecturers. Twelve years later, 554 Pennsylvania subordinates had 19 women Masters, 211 women Secretaries, and 241 women Lecturers; after another twelve years, in 1918, 881 Pennsylvania subordinates had 38 women Masters, 416 women Secretaries, and 508 women Lecturers.[52] These few numbers at least suggest a general trend. The proportion of women Masters grew modestly; the proportion of women Secretaries increased from about one-fourth to nearly one-half; and the proportion of women Lecturers grew from about one-fifth to a majority, about 57 percent, in 1918.

Other states distributed local offices in a broadly similar way. In 1888, for example, Connecticut's sixty-one subordinate Granges had no women Masters, five women Secretaries, and thirty-two women Lecturers.[53] Two years later, a New Hampshire woman observed that almost 40 percent of the Lecturers and Secretaries in her state were women, and in 1901, Kenyon Butterfield, who had edited Michigan's Grange journal before he became president of the Rhode Island, Michigan and Massachusetts agricultural colleges, estimated that a majority of local Grange Lecturers throughout the country were women. Butterfield also thought that Lecturers were the "most important" Grange officers after Masters, and the New Hampshire woman thought that the high proportion of women Secretaries and Lecturers in her state meant that "nearly half of the work requiring accuracy, honesty, and business and literary ability is done by women."[54]

Certainly, Secretaries and Lecturers had to do a great deal of demanding, responsible work. Some informed observers guessed that women were allowed to assume a big share of those offices for exactly that reason.[55] Lecturers, as Butterfield suggested, had an especially vital job—they planned and helped to conduct programs. If Grangers found their meetings dull, that was their Lecturers' fault. Recognizing the office's importance, the 1897 National Grange recommended that state Lecturers hold conferences to consider ways of improving Lecture work throughout the Order. Three conferences met in 1898, and then county, state, and regional conferences proliferated. In 1949, Grange historian Charles Gardner reported that the New England conference, which began in 1912, had become a four-day event that attracted up to 1,500 Patrons. It furnished a model for other regional conferences.[56] The Order also tried to help Lecturers by publishing helpful suggestions for programs. Mortimer Whitehead, a particularly active National Grange Lecturer who served from 1877 to 1878 and from 1886 to 1893, produced a series of leaflets that could have served as model lectures. One undated example, which also appeared in New York's Grange journal in 1888, was a speech by Flora Kimball, a prominent California Granger, on the splendid opportunities that the Grange was providing for women. Another leaflet from the National Grange Lecture Department was a collection of lofty thoughts about women that had appeared in various Grange documents. They may have furnished inspiring texts for lectures.[57]

Other Grange publications also supplied ideas for Lecturer's programs. For example, the "Home Department" of *National Grange* magazine published a list of topics for lectures and discussions, along with extensive reading lists, in 1910. Under "Home Ideals," the Department suggested programs on how best to spend Sundays, how attractive homes would help to keep young people on the farm, and "What effect has the beautiful on us, and how may we introduce it into our homes and lives?" The accompanying bibliography for that set of topics included Charlotte Perkins Gilman's *Woman and Economics*, a pioneering feminist work.[58] Not content with such occasional suggestions, some state Granges furnished subordinate Lecturers with handbooks outlining programs for a year at a time. Ohio's 1913 *Lecturer's Handbook* offered balanced programs, always with something that would interest the brothers and something else for the sisters. The first of two February meetings, for example, was to have a talk on cooperative business and another on household utensils. Whoever conducted the second lecture or discussion was advised to read a pamphlet by Martha Van Rensselaer, Cornell's famous home economist. The second meeting in July was to include consideration of potato spraying, the value of county experiment farms, "The Country Church," and "What can the Sisters of this Grange do to improve our Community?" Such suggestions would certainly have given Lecturers a general sense of direction, but without relieving them of any large part of their work. Local Lecturers had to study the recommended materials, plan discussions and write talks, or get other people to do those things. Preparing two of the solid, instructive programs that the Ohio State Grange wanted every month would have been a formidable task for anyone who had other work to do.[59]

Jennie Buell published a similar *Lecturer's Bulletin* during her service as Lecturer of the Michigan State Grange, from 1909 through 1913. She later conducted a column for Lecturers in the *National Grange Monthly*, and finally gathered her ideas together in a substantial book, *The Grange Master and the Grange Lecturer*. The second office had changed, she thought, since the Order's beginning. Early Lecturers really had lectured, but the "duties have since changed from those of a 'lecturer' to those of a teacher." Buell explained that the transformed Lecturer "must know people as well as facts; she must know how to arouse the indifferent members; she must tactfully draw out the stored-up funds in the non-communicative members; and she must incite to competition and rivalry those who are not moved by finer motives." In other words, the Lecturer had become less an authority and more a manager of human relations. Other observers made the same point. In 1898, an Illinois woman described a perfect Lecturer who discovered that a sister was staying away from meetings because she had only one really presentable dress, which was a funereal black. "Said the Lecturer, in her happy way, 'Your face and good words have a peculiar way of illuminating your clothes. I never knew your dress was black.' "[60] At the same time that Lecturers' responsibilities were changing, Buell reflected, the Order had "gradually seen women supplant men to a very great extent in this office in subordinate Granges." Buell merely put the two changes side by side, without attempting to show a relationship between men and authoritative Lecturers on one hand and women and tactful teachers on the other.[61]

Despite the feminization of the Lecturers' office, Buell thought that it retained "power" and "responsibility." The Lecturer shaped members' "ideals concerning their home and farm surroundings, rural schools, and local community conditions" and was "somewhat responsible for the attitude which the members hold toward issues . . . such as taxation, the land question, conservation of natural resources, transportation, rural school improvement, control of packers, collective bargaining" and other large questions of the day. Ideally, Buell suggested, the Lecturer would exercise her "power" indirectly. Rather than speaking much, she would simply call members' attention to the great questions, draw out their ideas, and always remember to be "thankful" for their contributions. Her task was very much like teaching in an ungraded school, where the pupils' ages and educational backgrounds varied widely. Buell knew that the "trained teacher, accustomed to dealing with grades and systems adapted to similar ages and stages of intellectual attainment, stands aghast at the situation confronting her when chosen Lecturer of a subordinate Grange." But she thought that the job was even more challenging for Lecturers who had not been teachers.[62]

By the time Buell described the Lecturer's task, women's participation in the Grange had expanded much beyond the very limited roles that the founders devised. Beginning with almost purely ornamental offices, women had moved into positions of real leadership. But even when Buell wrote about Lecturers, Grange equality was still, in the phrase Anson Bartlett used in an 1868 letter to Oliver Hudson Kelley, "varied . . . to suit the condition of the sexes."[63] Outside of a few weak Grange states, women rarely served as Masters. They were mainly Secretaries and Lecturers, and the Lecturers' office had changed as women took possession of it.

Buell's reflections on Lecturers are highly suggestive of the specialized kind of leadership that women exercised in their Granges, the effects that it had—or was supposed to have—on the conduct of Grange meetings, and the sorts of women who served as leaders. Buell's ideal woman leader was articulate, widely informed, and had pedagogical training or experience. Buell herself fit that description and it applied, very generally, to most of the other women who helped to lead the Grange.

NOTES

1. Oliver Hudson Kelley, *Origin and Progress of the Patrons of Husbandry in the United States: A History from 1866 to 1873* (Philadelphia: J. A. Wagenseller, 1875),

14–15; Woods, *Knights of the Plow*, 89–90; Lynn Dumenil, *Freemasonry and American Culture, 1880–1930* (Princeton: Princeton University Press, 1984), 7, 25–26.

2. Dumenil, *Freemasonry*, 14–16.

3. Mary Ann Clawson, *Constructing Brotherhood: Class, Gender, and Fraternalism* (Princeton: Princeton University Press, 1989), 4, 14, 185, 243.

4. Kelley, *Origin and Progress*, 16; Woods, *Knights of the Plow*, 92–93.

5. Nordin, *Rich Harvest*, 6; Woods, *Knights of the Plow*, 99–100 leaves no doubt that Kelley was the real founder and that Saunders, while the "dominating influence" among the Washington Grangers, had no constructive role in the "real organizational work" of the Order, which "did not really begin until Kelley" returned to Minnesota.

6. Clippings in Saunders scrapbooks, National Grange Records, Cornell University; Howard S. Miller, "Elizabeth Rowell Thompson" in *Notable American Women* (Cambridge: Harvard University Press, 1971), 3:452–54.

7. Robert Leslie Jones, *History of Agriculture in Ohio to 1880* (Kent: Kent State University Press, 1983), 188.

8. Kelley, *Origin and Progress*, 24–25; *Constitution of the Patrons of Husbandry*, 1868, does not list the graces as officers; *Manual and Monitor of Subordinate Granges, of the Patrons of Husbandry* (St. Paul: National Grange, 1869), 51–53 prescribes installation rites for the graces and the Stewardess (later Lady Assistant Steward) along with the other officers.

9. Kelley, *Origin and Progress*, 55–57.

10. Ibid., 71–75.

11. Ralph W. Smith, *History of the Iowa State Grange* (Manchester: Iowa State Grange, 1946), 25; *Manual and Monitor*, 17–18; C. Jerome Davis, High Priest of Demeter, emeritus, writes that the ninth edition of the manual was the first to print only combined versions of the first four degrees, rather than continuing to offer separate ceremonies for men and women as options. His copy of the ninth edition was printed in 1906. Davis, Ramsey, Indiana, to Marti, 6 June 1988.

12. *Dedication of Grange Halls Adopted By The National Grange at the Ninth Annual Session* (Louisville: National Grange, 1875). It may be too easy for outsiders to dismiss fraternal ritual as meaningless play. In fact, it may be deeply meaningful play. Nick Salvatore, *Eugene V. Debs: Citizens and Socialist* (Urbana: University of Illinois Press, 1982), 26 suggests that the railroad firemen's lodge ritual "could strengthen a feeling of solidarity, and it held within itself the seeds of a potent opposition to the highly competitive ethos of American society."

13. Kelley, *Origin and Progress*, 24, 77.

14. Aaron B. Grosh, *Mentor in the Granges and Homes of Patrons of Husbandry* (New York: Clark and Maynard, 1876), 124.

15. Wisconsin State Grange *Bulletin* 4 (May 1878).

16. *Farmers' Friend and Grange Advocate* 22 (7 September 1895): 5.

17. *Pennsylvania Grange News* 5 (February 1909 supplement), 10.

18. *National Grange* 1 (20 November 1907): 11.

19. Minutes of Olive Grange No. 189, 15 June 1889, 21 December 1889, and undated 1891 entry, Indiana Historical Society.

20. Atkeson, *Semi-Centennial History of the Patrons of Husbandry*, 377–48; Eliza

C. Gifford, address to the New York State Grange, February 1894, in Gifford manuscripts, Patterson Library and Art Gallery.

21. Marie Howland, Hammonton, 19 January 1876, to William Saunders, in National Grange Records, Cornell University Library.

22. *Proceedings of the Eighth Annual Session of the State Grange of New Jersey* (Woodstown: State Grange, 1880), 10; Hebb, "The Woman Movement in the California State Grange," 30; Neth, "Building the Base," 339 argues that women built the social foundations of twentieth-century midwestern farm organizations. Planning entertainments and serving meals were essential parts of this.

23. *Constitution of the Patrons of Husbandry*, 1868, 4.

24. *Minnesota Monthly* 1 (March 1869): 97–98.

25. D. Wyatt Aiken, *The Grange, Its Origin, Progress and Educational Purposes* (Washington: National Grange, 1883), 6–7.

26. Dolores Hayden, *The Grand Domestic Revolution: A History of Feminist Designs for American Homes, Neighborhoods, and Cities* (Cambridge: MIT Press, 1981), 101; *Journal of Proceedings of the Twelfth Annual Session of the National Grange of the Patrons of Husbandry*, 1878, 77.

27. Mildred Throne, "The Grange in Iowa, 1868–1875," *Iowa Journal of History* 47 (October 1949): 298–99; Woods, *Knights of the Plow*, 150–51 has tables showing the proliferation of subordinate Granges in 1873 and 1874.

28. *Indiana Farmer* 12 (10 March 1877): 7.

29. Kelley, *Origin and Progress*, 24–25; *Constitution of the Patrons of Husbandry*, 1868; *Manual and Monitor*, 51–53; *Constitution of the Patrons of Husbandry*, 1873, 6, 9–10.

39. Grosh, *Mentor*, 119.

31. *The Husbandman* 1 (31 March 1875): 4.

32. Hebb, "The Woman Movement in the California State Grange," 36, 38.

33. *Constitution of the Patrons of Husbandry*, 1873, 7.

34. *Report of Proceedings of the Sixth Annual Session of the Iowa State Grange* (Des Moines: State Grange, 1875), 36–39.

35. *Proceedings of the State Grange of Wisconsin* (Oshkosh: State Grange, 1874), 10–12; Robert C. Nesbit, *The History of Wisconsin* (Madison: State Historical Society of Wisconsin, 1985), 3: 461.

36. *Journal of Proceedings of the Ninth Session of the National Grange*, 1875, 53.

37. Kelley, *Origin and Progress*, 143.

38. *Proceedings of the Third Annual Session of the Connecticut State Grange, 1887* (Hartford: State Grange, 1888).

39. *Grange Visitor* 12 (15 December 1887): 5.

40. *National Grange* 4 (28 June 1909): 3.

41. *Penn State Alumni News* 18 (February 1932): 6.

42. *Journal of Proceedings of the National Grange*, 1901, 72.

43. Ms. letter to subordinate and Pomona Grange Lecturers from Clara L. Williams, 1924 (?), in Archives of the Maryland State Grange, Special Collections, University of Maryland College Park Libraries.

44. *The Husbandman* 1 (31 March 1875): 4.

45. *The Indiana Farmer* 12 (10 March 1877): 7; Hebb, "The Woman Movement in the California State Grange," 39.

46. Smith, *The History of the Iowa State Grange*, 22; *Report of Proceedings of the Sixth Annual Session of the Iowa State Grange*, 1875, 10–11.

47. Rosters of state officers in National Grange *Proceedings* from 1879 through 1895.

48. Rosters in National Grange *Proceedings* from 1895 through 1920.

49. Rosters in National Grange *Proceedings* from 1900 through 1920.

50. Rosters in National Grange *Proceedings* from 1879 through 1920.

51. Rosters in National Grange *Proceedings* from 1879 through 1920.

52. *Register of State, Pomona, and Subordinate Grange Officers* (Mechanicsburg: Pennsylvania State Grange, 1894), with similar registers for 1906 and 1918 in the Pennsylvania State Grange office.

53. *Official Directory of Connecticut Patrons of Husbandry* (Putnam: State Grange, 1888).

54. *Journal of Proceedings Seventeenth Annual Session of the New Hampshire State Grange, 1890* (Concord: State Grange, 1891), 81–82; Kenyon Butterfield, "The Grange," *The Forum* 31 (April 1901): 233.

55. Bertels, "The National Grange: Progressives on the Land, 1900–1930," 94–95.

56. Gardner, *The Grange*, 412–14; Nordin, *Rich Harvest*, 39 cites an 1875 complaint by the Master of the South Carolina State Grange about the difficulty of preparing attractive programs for meetings. The Master thought that their inability to meet that challenge had killed many local Granges.

57. Leaflets 1 and 6 from the National Grange Lecture Department are available, with others, in the National Agricultural Library. Number 1 also appeared in *The Husbandman* 14 (11 January 1888): 3.

58. National Grange 5 (16 February 1910): 6.

59. L. J. Taber, *Lecturers Handbook* (N.p.: Ohio State Grange, 1913), 10, 20.

60. *American Grange Bulletin and Scientific Farmer* 26 (12 October 1899): 10–11.

61. Jennie Buell, *The Grange Master and the Grange Lecturer* (New York: Harcourt, Brace and Company, 1921), vii, 96–97.

62. Ibid., 99–101, 134.

63. Kelley, *Origin and Progress*, 71–75.

2

Teachers, Farmers, and Famous Grangers

The women who held Grange offices and contributed to the Order's programs and publications varied in obvious ways. Most of them farmed, but a substantial minority did not. Many were "prominent" and "well-off," as a local historian described the founders of one Minnesota Grange. Others were small, landowning, commercial farmers or were modestly prosperous townspeople. A handful of them achieved regional or national fame; thousands more were notable only in their local Granges. A few ventured radical criticisms of American society, and especially of its ordinary gender relationships; more were generally conventional but deeply committed to women's rights; and another large group focused on women's domestic concerns. The leaders were far from homogeneous, but they varied within a limited social and cultural range. They were mostly middle-class, self-consciously modern, Protestant, native-born Americans. Although they were especially concerned about women's problems, they refused to be confined to women's offices and subjects. Their biographies and inferences that can be drawn from their pronouncements about the Order illustrate their differences and shared attributes.[1]

Those inferences are helpful because Grange women rarely wrote about themselves directly or in any detail. A few described their work, or complained about some problem, but they did not provide facts about their educations, religious experiences and affiliations, marriages, or economic situations. Often, in contributing to Grange journals, they refused even to say who they were. That reticence, and the indifference of local historians, journalists, and others who might have written about them, makes biographical information about all but a few Grange women difficult or impossible to come by. Even really notable women, like Sallie J. Back, who was Lecturer of the Indiana State Grange from 1881 through 1886—when women rarely held such lofty positions—have disappeared with little trace. Historians of women are all too familiar with such disappearances. Having tried to learn about similarly elusive individuals, the author of a recent dissertation reports that only sketchy documentation exists for all but a few Alliance and Populist women. Some left "only a name," dates when they held offices, or announcements of speeches.[2] The same can be said of many Grangers, including a few who wrote enough to suggest that they would have been rewarding to study. But some of the sisters made revealing, if indirect, statements about themselves in the course of writing about the Order.

For example, Lida Clark, a New York Grange woman, produced an essay entitled "Why Are Women in the Granges?" in 1875. She reported that the Order had been criticized for admitting women and that an especially vehement newspaper writer had condemned Grangers for letting women impersonate Ceres, Pomona, and Flora. He was shocked that presumably Christian women were disporting themselves as pagan divinities. Clark defended the graces, arguing that they stood for values that Christianity had not superceded, and then paid an extended tribute to classical culture. Her essay allows the inference that she was an educated person who admired the ancients and enjoyed an argument. Enthusiasm for the classics was a little unusual among Grangers, though Mary Mayo once lectured her county Grange about Socrates and his wife Xanthippe.[3] But the other parts of what Lida Clark said about herself were not unusual at all.

Grange women found many ways to assert their intelligence and cultural ambition. Throughout the last quarter of the nineteenth century, they called for less attention to cookery in the Ladies' Departments of Grange journals, or said that cooking was important but should not be allowed to distract women from more intellectual pursuits. They turned discussions of child-rearing immediately to education and blessed the Grange for encouraging farm people to live graciously. Sisters who had little time for writing, or who found it difficult, showed ambition when they composed a few lines for the Grange, as did more fluent women who turned out flowery poems, elaborately ornamented essays, and vigorous arguments.

Many of them also found ways to say that they had strong moral commitments. Sarah Baird made that very clear in 1909, the fourteenth year of her service as Master of the Minnesota State Grange, when she thanked the editors of the *National Grange* for their superior work. She observed that "ordinary papers" were full of "murders, robberies, wife beaters, drunken and depraved boys killing parents, divorces and the like," while the *National Grange* was a "clean, pure paper, with its pure news of the world and our Order, without a single bloodcurdling crime, but holding aloft the torchlight of purity and truth."[4] Another woman, just as outspokenly devoted to purity, told her Wisconsin sisters that their influence had kept the brothers from bringing their crude, masculine ways into the Grange. Many others rejoiced that the Order had enlisted their influence to foster gentility and temperance.[5]

Grange women also showed that they were religious, which was hardly surprising. The Order forbade potentially divisive religious discussions in Grange meetings, but a highly generalized religiosity was part of its ethos. Pennsylvania's state Grange Lecturer demonstrated its importance in 1889 when he praised the Order's "religious but unsectarian character" and reported that many local Granges "throw open their halls for Sabbath-schools and public worship."[6] A woman made the same point in a 1914 talk to Erie County, Pennsylvania, Grangers. "The church people are found active in the grange," she observed with great satisfaction, and "the grange people are found active in the church." In her neighborhood, the two institutions cemented their alliance each year when Grangers marched to the neighborhood church together.[7]

Women honored the Order's ban on religious controversy by saying very little about their particular faiths, but a Pennsylvania sister devoted her speech at the big Williams Grove picnic of 1892 to a brief appreciation of Christianity's social benefits and a much longer attack on the subjugation of women in the church. After some preliminary attention to St. Paul and Martin Luther, she considered the "last General Conference of the Methodist Episcopal Church," which had refused to admit women as delegates. That denomination was in the midst of a protracted battle about women's status, which the offended sister assumed was of some interest to her Grange audience. It probably was. Given the well-attested fact that Grangers recruited few Catholics, Lutherans, and very conservative evangelicals, it was reasonable for her to think that the people gathered at Williams Grove had some interest in mainline Protestant denominations.[8]

Finally, a Wisconsin woman who chose to call herself "Folly" made an explicit point about her sisters' backgrounds and, implicitly, described her own. She observed that discussions of education in her Grange tended to be long and spirited because six of the women members, which was probably "a small average for Granges throughout the state," had been teachers. Her number would have meant more if she had said how many women belonged to her Grange, but six women who were accustomed to standing in front of classrooms must surely have had an effect on its meetings. Most women teachers lost their opportunity to speak with authority when they married; having settled down to obscure domesticity, they may have welcomed the new sort of classroom that the Grange offered. "Folly's" observation, the frequency with which Grange women discussed education, and the wealth of teaching experience among notable women Grangers suggest that they did.[9]

More can be learned about leading Grange women from a handful of well-documented lives. The available examples include a few early leaders who were politically radical, personally unconventional, and fiercely devoted to women's rights; never representative of the Order's leadership, they had no real successors in the Grange, but they illustrate some of its characteristics in particularly striking ways. Some of them were active in California, where an historian reports that the early Granges attracted individuals who "had their own 'rows to hoe' " and that some of them were women's rights advocates who hoped to enlist the Order in their cause.[10] Similarly, the Secretary of the Pennsylvania State Grange, speaking to a women's suffrage organization in 1894, recalled suffragists in his region who "saw in the Grange the means and opportunity for disseminating suffrage doctrine." "At first their opinions and doctrines, and the more particularly the voicing of them, were strong meat for the farmers' wives and daughters," but they made a lasting impact. He remembered a few especially interesting individuals who became valuable Grangers. One was Marie Howland of New Jersey.[11]

Howland was born in Lebanon, New Hampshire, in 1836 and moved to Lowell, Massachusetts, when her father died. Though only twelve years old, she supported herself and her younger twin sisters by working thirteen hours a day in a textile mill. Hard labor and boarding house life, according to present-day admirers, taught her "both independence and co-operation," while instilling the "independent industrial worker's contempt for the idle, middle-class women who thought of themselves as virtuous 'ladies,' "[12] She worked in the mills for two years and then moved to New York City, where she probably failed as an actress, taught in the Five Points slum, and attended a normal school at night. She became principal of a city school in 1857, when she married Lyman W. Case. The couple lived among radicals, including Stephen Pearl Andrews, who helped Victoria Woodhull and Tennessee Claflin to found their notorious journal, in a cooperative rooming house with elements of a Fourierist phalanstery. When she was attracted to Edward Howland, a Harvard graduate who had escaped from his father's cotton brokerage to radical journalism, Case graciously insisted that she follow her new inclination. She did. After spending the Civil War years in Europe, she returned to the United States with a divorce from Case and a new marriage to Howland.[13]

The Howlands settled on a farm near Hammontown, New Jersey, in 1882. Edward was no farmer, so Marie did most of the work and also brightened the place with fifty kinds of roses. In return, he beautified the house by painting wise sayings on the doors and walls. The kitchen cupboard announced, " 'Sine Cerere et Bacho, Friget Venus' " (Without Ceres and Bacchus, or food and wine, Venus, or love, grows cold). Casa Tonti, as they cryptically called their home, was a radical salon regularly visited by old friends from the city, a center of New Jersey's nascent Grange movement, and certainly an exceptional farm.[14]

The Howlands were as unlikely Grangers as they were farmers. He "hated secret societies" and often forgot the secret unwritten work, but they embraced the Order, as she explained in an 1873 magazine article, because "we may hope that this is the great moving army of the people so long waited for, which is to work out the vexed problems of labor and capital by a sudden and peaceful revolution."[15] New Jersey's part of the army was small enough to provide leadership opportunities for hopeful radicals; in June 1873, the state had only three subordinate Granges, one of them founded at Casa Tonti. So Edward Howland became Master of the New Jersey State Grange, which started that year, and Marie Howland was Ceres; the two represented the Garden State at the 1874 National Grange. That year's *Proceedings* say little about their contributions, but Master Howland informed his own state organization that "the recognition of women . . . and their serving on committees . . . was due chiefly to your sister representative from New Jersey." A decade later, he recalled that she had "surprised members [of the National Grange] by sitting at the same tables as the men rather than at a separate set of benches for women at the side of the room."[16] She had made a difference, of which her husband was publicly and lastingly proud.

In 1876, Marie Howland expressed some discontent with the Order, especially with its devotion to cooperative enterprises. She told William Saunders, the first Master of the National Grange who had left the Order late in 1875 after Kelley moved its headquarters from Washington to Kentucky, that the "grange will never rally from the commercial incubus that now sits upon it." Her own Grange stressed education, mainly through informal discussions, but she thought that the Order in general was becoming "a mere business caucus." That would alienate women, Howland thought; it was certainly disappointing her own hopes for the Order. Then she happily told Saunders about more promising developments. "That communistic movement in Russia is wonderful," she observed, and New York had a splendid florescence of new reform societies.[17]

When the Howlands moved on to new radical ventures, as they seem to have done very quickly, nobody quite assumed their venturesome role in the Order. Augusta Cooper Bristol may have come closest. Born in Croydon, New Hampshire, in 1835, Bristol attended two academies, and began to teach and publish poetry when she was fifteen years old. She married seven years later, divorced five years after that, and then married again in 1866. After a few years in southern Illinois, where she gave her first public lecture and published a volume of poems, the Bristols settled in Vineland, New Jersey. There she gave monthly "lessons from Spencer and Carey" to the Ladies' Social Science class for four years and, in 1880, presented a series of lectures to the New York Positivist Society on "The Evolution of Character." Soon after that, she spent several months in Guise, France, where Jean Baptiste Andrew Godin had organized an iron foundry on Fourierist principles. She also lectured on the "Scientific Basis of Morality" at a "convention of liberal thinkers" in Brussels. Bristol gave the nominating speech for Benjamin Butler at the 1884 Greenback convention, toured California speaking for women's suffrage and, at various times, took friendly interests in Transcendentalism, Spiritualism, Christian Science, and Vineland's Congregational and Unitarian churches. Soon after returning to New Jersey from Europe, Bristol became Lecturer of her local Grange in Vineland and of the New Jersey State Grange. The National Grange also employed her as a traveling speaker. Women Lecturers were still unusual in the early 1880s, but Bristol came to the job with exceptional experience.[18]

Clarina Irene Howard Nichols, a wide-ranging reformer and dedicated suffragist, was another distinctive presence in the early Grange. Born in West Townshend, Vermont, in 1810, Nichols studied in district schools and, for one year, in a select school and then married in 1830. She and her husband moved to western New York, where she is thought to have founded a seminary for young women. She moved back to Vermont in 1839, probably without her husband, started writing for the *Windham County Democrat*, divorced her first husband, and married the *Democrat*'s editor. Becoming editor herself, Nichols filled the paper with advocacy of abolition, prohibition, Fourierism, and other reforms. One of her editorials concerned married women's legal and economic disabilities. She also lectured. After her second husband died, Nichols moved west, first to Kansas where she campaigned for equal suffrage in 1867, and then to California. A charter member of her local Grange, which she frequently instructed about women's rights, Nichols also wrote in favor of equal suffrage for Grange publications. In 1881, she jubilantly informed *Pacific Rural Press* readers that Vermont had given women the right to vote in school elections. She remembered presenting a petition to the Vermont legislature asking for that very reform twenty-eight years earlier.[19]

Howland, Bristol, and Nichols had some very general attributes in common with other Grange leaders. They were more than ordinarily well-educated, convinced that people and society were capable of improvement, and intellectually ambitious. They had all been teachers, which was a common element in the experience of women Grange leaders. But not many Grangers were divorced, Fourierist, Positivist, revolutionary, or resident in New Jersey. Howland, Bristol, and Nichols really were exceptional leaders. Most of the committed suffragists who brought their reforming fervor to the early Grange were much more conventional women. Jeanne C. Carr and Flora Kimball, two of the most important leaders in the early California Granges, are prominent and well-documented examples.

Born in 1823, Carr was the oldest daughter of a Vermont physician and heir to a religious tradition that combined, as she liked to think, the "straitest puritan lineage" with a spirit of toleration. She was deeply proud of her heritage and of missionary relatives, including a sister who died in Turkey. Her own life was less adventurous. She married Dr. Ezra Carr, a graduate of the Castleton Medical College, when she was only eighteen years old, and then followed his academic career westward. The Carrs reached California in 1869, four years ahead of the Grange.[20]

Jeanne Carr represented the Vacaville and Pleasant Valley Fruit Association at the April 1873 Farmers' Union convention that decided to found a state Grange. Then she served the Grange itself in various capacities. Carr was a member of its committee on education and labor in 1874, when she introduced resolutions favoring practical, vocational training in all schools through the state university and addressed a meeting of state Grange women on dress reform in 1875. As she warned in advance, her talk on clothing featured a "full set of all the newly invented hygienic under garments for women and children" modeled by a large doll. In 1876, she became the first woman to run for one of the working offices of the California State Grange. Women Lecturers were still unusual even at the local level, but Carr lost the contest for state Lecturer only on the third ballot. She became Chaplain in 1877 and Lecturer in 1879. Carr also testified in favor of equal suffrage before a committee of California's 1878 constitutional convention and then helped to keep the issue before the Grange. In 1876, she told the women members of the state Grange, assembled apart from their husbands, that the Grange might be the " 'entering wedge' to shatter the false system of laws that has so oppressed women for all time." Douglas Hebb calls Carr "by far the leading feminist associated with the California Grange."[21]

She may have been, if allowances are made for the anachronism of using the word "feminist" a generation ahead of its time, but Flora Kimball was another women's rights advocate who made a forceful impact on California Granges. Kimball was born in Warner, New Hampshire, in 1829, attended local schools, and taught from the age of fifteen until she married Warren G. Kimball in 1857. Kimball and his brothers were entrepreneurial builders who moved to San Francisco in 1861 and developed National City, just outside of San Diego, in 1870. They suffered business reversals shortly before Flora Kimball died in 1898, but she enjoyed wealth and civic prominence through most of her life in National City. She was a school trustee for eight years, "invariably" spent one afternoon a week visiting the schools and entertaining children at her showplace home, helped to found a public library, and supported a wide range of other social, cultural, and religious improvements. Devoted to women's rights since early youth, Kimball belonged to state and local women's suffrage organizations, the Woman's Parliament, and National Ranch Grange in National City. Elected Master in 1878, she was probably the first woman to hold that office in any California Grange. She was certainly among the earliest women Masters in the country.[22]

Her Grange work included writing for several journals that served the Order. She wrote essays and letters, as did many other Grange women, as well as fiction, which showed exceptional ambition. One of her contributions to the *California Patron* was a short story that began with a farm woman weeping in outrage because of a newspaper item that described women as consumers, like "idlers, aristocrats, and vagabonds," who depended on other people's production. Her husband, trying to calm her, said that she exaggerated the insult's importance because she was tired from her hard day's work. The woman really was tired but replied that she "could do a dozen washings with greater ease than to find myself taunted in every newspaper paragraph that I read, with being a woman!" Meanwhile, her husband worried that the farm might fail, and their older daughter, sensing his fear, resolved to support herself by teaching. Kimball then assured her readers that although men often wonder how the "frail vines that cling" to them will bear their failures, "clinging vines" are apt to be unexpectedly strong. The mother and daughter in her story were entirely capable of hard work and independence. They deserved respect, which was just what the mother felt that women were too regularly denied.[23]

Kimball claimed that the Grange honored women by including them as members and taking their work seriously. It affirmed "the old-time theory" that women's work centers on the home, invested the domestic sphere with dignity, and encouraged women in "every worthy cause that has for its object the strengthening of domestic ties and the improvement of our dwelling places." While treating their home responsibilities respectfully, the Grange also taught women that "the word home has a broader significance than the four walls within which we eat, sleep, and mingle together." Properly understood, as Kimball claimed that it was in the Grange, women's domestic work included community and national reform.[24] That understanding was perfectly commonplace in the Grange, as it was in women's clubs and the WCTU. Kimball's teaching experience and cultural ambition were also typical of many women Grange leaders. But her distance from farming, and her status as the great lady of National City, distinguished Kimball from her sisters.

More typical Grange women, who lived and worked on farms, were just as strongly committed to women's rights. For example, Eliza C. Gifford, a Chautauqua County, New York, farm woman, campaigned for equal suffrage as persistently as any woman in the Order. One of five children born to yankee farmers who had both taught, Gifford attended a select school for two terms, spent another two terms at Jamestown Academy, and then taught intermittently for seven years before she married at the age of twenty-two. She later recalled her satisfaction at being told that she "taught the best School" that some community "had ever had," but then asked her audience to imagine, "if you can, what had been the quality of their schools!" She had been a young, inexperienced pedagogue, but doubtless worth the $2.75 a week "with board round the district" that her employers paid.[25] Then she married, raised six children, and helped her husband to look after his inherited farm, which prospered in their care. The Giffords also shared civic careers that included prominent roles in the Grange.

Walter Gifford helped to organize cooperative fire insurance companies, served two terms in the state legislature, organized Chautauqua County Granges as a deputy for the state Grange and, finally, served as Master of the state Grange from 1890 to 1894. Both Giffords were charter members of Union Grange No. 244. Master of that unit and of the Chautauqua County Pomona Grange, Eliza Gifford wrote for Grange publications and participated in both state and national Grange meetings. She proposed an equal suffrage resolution to the New York State Grange in 1881, kept the issue before the Order for more than twenty years after that, and also worked for equal suffrage through the WCTU, the Chautauqua Country Woman Suffrage Association, and the New York State Woman Suffrage Association. The Giffords seem to have been Methodists; nothing in her surviving writings indicates a strong interest in the church, but her WCTU activities and praise of the Grange as one of the "Christianizing forces of the age" epitomize its optimistic faith.[26]

Another Chautauqua County farm woman, closely allied with Eliza Gifford, also achieved prominence in the Grange. Carrie E. S. Twing, who lived near Westfield, was particularly distinguished as a Grange speaker. She lectured throughout the northeastern states and, like Gifford, participated in the WCTU and suffrage organizations. Also like Gifford, she taught in her youth, attended an academy, and married a successful farmer; her 1910 obituary in the local newspaper described him as a "well known vineyardist." Far more active and unconventional in religion than most Grange women, Twing preached Spiritualism and served as President of the New York State Spiritualist Association.[27]

Sarah C. Carpenter, who served as Chaplain of the Rhode Island State

Grange for a decade after its foundation in 1887, had a broadly similar career. Born in rural Cumberland, Rhode Island, in 1856, Carpenter attended public schools and the State Normal School in Providence and then taught for several years before she married George Carpenter, a notably progressive dairy farmer. She raised three children, superintended a Universalist Sunday school for thirty-three years, participated in her congregation's ladies' aid and the WCTU, and held various Grange offices. She regularly told Rhode Island Grangers that the Order existed to reform society. The two essential reforms of the day, she thought, were temperance and equal suffrage; the latter was prerequisite to the former.[28]

Sarah Baird, Master of the Minnesota State Grange for seventeen years beginning in 1895, and the first woman to head any state Grange, had much the same background. Born in Albany, Vermont, in 1842, Baird moved with her family to Minneapolis when she was fourteen years old, attended the town schools, graduated from a normal school in 1860, and taught until 1865, when she married George W. Baird. They farmed in Edina Mills, which is now Edina, one of the more affluent Minneapolis suburbs; the "modern steam-heated house" that they built in 1889 still stands on the now invisible boundary between city and suburb. Sometimes, before that house went up, Baird complained about the cold, and she was often tired from housework, cooking, churning, canning, gardening, and other chores. But even when she complained, Baird recognized that she was relatively fortunate. "If it is so hard for us to keep comfortable what of the poor," she asked her diary on a particularly frigid January day. Her advantages included a farm known for "top quality merino sheep," proximity to Minneapolis where she frequently visited her parents, and a lively circle of friends.[29]

The Bairds joined Minnehaha Grange No. 398 when it began in 1873. Edina's historian says that it was one of the original cultural institutions in the community. The others were the school and Trinity Chapel, which later became the Edina Congregational Church. The historian also reports that the twenty-one founders of Minnehaha Grange were "prominent, well-off farmers" who later allowed some other people, including the miller, to join their select group. They built a hall down by Minnehaha Creek, close to the Baird farm, where they enjoyed uplifting social and cultural activities. In 1874, one of them wrote that they hoped to "elevate, educate, and build up the Farmer to a standard that he may be recognized as a fit person for first society, which he now stands far beneath."[30] Baird contributed to its efforts by speaking, writing for the local Grange paper, and holding some office for about forty years. She was Master of the local Grange and Treasurer, Secretary, and Master of the state Grange.[31]

Unlike Elizabeth Gifford and other famous sisters, Baird showed little interest in equal suffrage. She valued the Grange, not as a political instrument, but because it promised to enrich farmers', especially farm women's, social and intellectual lives. Mary Mayo chose the same emphasis. One of only two women included among the 200 great agriculturists in Liberty Hyde Bailey's magisterial *Cyclopedia of American Agriculture* (1909), Mayo was the most widely known, and is now the most frequently remembered, Grange woman of the late nineteenth century. She had interests outside of the Grange, in the Methodist Episcopal Church and the Chautauqua Literary and Scientific Circle, but the Order absorbed most of the energy that she had to spare from her home. It made her famous.[32]

She was born in 1845, of an English mother and yankee father, on their farm near Battle Creek, Michigan. Her father's spinster sisters began her schooling, which continued through Battle Creek High School. Then she taught for five years, before marrying Perry Mayo, who had just returned from the Civil War, in 1865. Living in a two-room log cabin across the road from her childhood home, the young Mayos shared the hard work of developing their farm. Jennie Buell, who knew her well, wrote that "Mrs. Mayo was no one to shirk any task because it stood on the far side of the line custom had decreed was the boundary of 'woman's work.'" She worked in house, dairy, poultry yard, garden, and fields as necessary. The farm later prospered enough to relieve her of most outdoor tasks, but Jennie Buell thought that Mayo continued milking almost until she died in 1903. Milking was a relief from her other responsibilities; she told Buell that she prayed when she milked. She also had household chores that remained heavy even after a handsome frame house replaced the log cabin, and two children. Nelson, born in 1866, became a distinguished veterinarian; Nelly, born in 1872, required a great deal of her mother's attention when she lost a leg in 1890. Mayo wrote and spoke about farm women's hard work with real authority.[33]

She never complained about farm life but understood its problems. One, which forced itself on her attention early in her marriage, was especially troubling. Shopping in Battle Creek, she met a town woman, a former high school acquaintance, who expressed regret that Mayo had married a farmer. The condescending lady said that farm women could only "work hard and make lots of good butter." That stung Mayo. As she later told Jennie Buell, "I knew that I did work hard and that I made good butter, but it made me indignant to think that this was the measure of my life, and that of every farmer's wife." She and her husband responded to the slight by studying their old school books together and by seeking the company of neighbors who also wanted to lead a "cultured rural life."[34]

The Mayos' aspiration involved them in two organizations, the Grange and the Chautauqua Literary and Scientific Circle. The Circle was a home study program that began in 1878 as an extension of the assemblies that Dr. John Heyl Vincent, later a Methodist Bishop, had organized to improve the skills and general culture of Sunday school teachers. The Circle prescribed an ambitious series of readings that provided the substance of a college curriculum without foreign or ancient languages. Both Mayos completed the course; classes met at their home, under Mary Mayo's leadership, for five or six years. Chautauqua and Grange work mixed easily. Jennie Buell, who was active in both, arranged to have Mayo speak to at least one combined meeting of Grangers and Chautauquans.[35]

The Mayos joined the Grange at about the same time that they began the Chautauqua course. They first participated in their neighborhood unit, but she later recalled that it " 'did not strike me well at first, and I do not think it did Mr. Mayo. It was all for buying direct from the manufacturers. There was little that was educational about it, being scarcely more than a round of routine business.' " So the Mayos transferred to Battle Creek Grange, which offered lectures on a wide range of edifying topics. Soon they were also active in the county, or Pomona, Grange, which sent them to the 1882 state Grange. A woman who met them there observed that they were "young, active and full of Grange vim." She knew that Mary Mayo had begun to write for the *Visitor*, Michigan's Grange newspaper, and that both Mayos were "public speakers, so many of us may have the privilege of listening to them during the coming winter."[36]

Mary Mayo had broken into print by writing reports of Pomona Grange meetings for the *Grange Visitor* and contributing a brief essay to the *Visitor's* "Ladies' Department" in November 1880. At least hundreds of women wrote similar essays for comparable departments in Grange journals all over the country. She began her entirely unremarkable first effort by announcing that she had found a little leisure and felt that "we all owe our Grange organ to each send an article occasionally to its columns." Then she called attention to a recent article in *Scribner's Monthly*, which she believed was in the March issue, entitled "What Our Boys Are Reading." Too many were reading "sensational, blood and thunder trash," which would not do to produce "honest, temperate, Christian men." Boys needed "instructive reading matter every week."[37]

The impression that the Mayos were public speakers was based on their contributions to Farmers' Institutes, which were lecture series sponsored by state boards of agriculture and agricultural colleges. Mary Mayo presented what was probably her first Institute address in Marshall, which was not far from her home, in 1877. On "A Higher Standard of Culture for Housekeepers," it said that home is a cherished ideal, that woman is the "soul" of home, and that homes need "cultivated mothers." Most women lacked time to cultivate their minds, but they could make time if they would "dress plainer, eat plainer foods, and spend less time on outside show."[38] Mayo consistently emphasized that theme through the rest of her Grange career. Two years later, at a Battle Creek Institute, she returned to the value of intellectual culture with an address entitled "Does Education Lead to Extravagance?" She said that it did, very often, because too much education had nothing to do with preparing people to live competently and decently. Ancient languages and higher mathematics were useless, but people should learn how to do their work efficiently, nurture their children, and sustain right relations with God and other people. Education was a great blessing but only when it served moral and other practical purposes.[39]

Mayo's Grange speaking started in her own county, and then she ventured farther afield with her husband along for moral support. She always remembered her first long speaking trip, probably in 1882, when she traveled thirty-six miles to a Grange in Barry County where people "came just out of curiosity to hear a woman speak." Some were "indignant," others amused, and "just a few women . . . drank in eagerly what little I had to say."[40] In 1884, she had to "pluck up courage" to travel one county eastward by herself while her husband worked on the farm. Then she toured several counties for a week that summer as a deputy for the state Grange. Traveling every day, lecturing every night, and trying to enlist often indifferent people into the Order was hard, sometimes discouraging, work. But she gave "fifty lectures and several talks" in various places one year after that and gave seventy-three lectures in 1886. She battled "bad roads, rough weather, late trains, weariness, and homesickness" to strengthen the Order. She also served by chairing the Michigan State Grange committee on woman's work for fourteen years, promoting annual children's days in the Grange, and organizing fresh air projects, which brought urban women and children to Grange farms for summer outings. Pomona of the state Grange in 1887, she served as Deputy Lecturer from 1888 until she died in 1903 and as Chaplain for much of that period.[41]

Mayo was never active in the equal suffrage campaign. Like Sarah Baird, she demonstrated that a prominent, vocal Grange woman could all but ignore political issues of every kind. Her husband was a Republican state legislator and sometimes led Grange discussions of public questions, but Mayo stayed clear of such matters. She once told *Visitor* readers that she approved of a Republican candidate for Governor because he was a good man and favored prohibition, but that was exceptional for her.[42] Uncritical of the conventional division of responsibility between men and women, she focused on domesticity and left politics to her husband. That set Mayo apart from Carr, Kimball, Gifford, and other important Grange leaders. But Sarah Baird and many of the relatively obscure women who spoke in Grange meetings and wrote for

Grange journals followed the same course. They considered domesticity a sufficiently important subject, especially for rural women who had not attained what Grange women considered its highest possibilities.

Mayo's career in the Michigan State Grange overlapped with those of two other famous women leaders, who also happened to be Michiganders. Olivia Woodman, who succeeded Mayo as Chaplain of the state Grange and held that office until she died in 1929, was born on a New York farm in 1847. Educated at an academy in Lansing, Michigan, she taught before being ordained as a Universalist minister in 1895. Not yet married, she was active in the state Grange, served on its education committee and, in 1892, got the body to adopt a resolution opposing school consolidation. She married Jonathan J. Woodman, a widower and past Master of the state and national Granges, in 1897, but that did not interrupt her ministry or reform activities. She was President of her county's equal suffrage association, represented the state Grange on the board of Michigan's anti-saloon league, and spoke for conservation, municipal government reforms, and restrictions on child labor. The Grange shared her organizational loyalties with the Order of the Eastern Star, the Ladies of the Maccabees, and both local and state federations of women's clubs.[43]

A younger contemporary, Jennie Buell, became probably the best-known Grange woman in the first third of this century. Born in rural southwestern Michigan in 1863, Buell attended local schools, graduated from the normal school at Ypsilanti, and neither farmed nor married after she left her parents' home. Her Grange prominence began when J. T. Cobb, who was Secretary of the state Grange and editor of the *Grange Visitor*, asked the young woman to write for his journal. Sharing Cobb's editorial and secretarial work, Buell became a regular contributor to the *Visitor*, and then served as state Grange Secretary from 1890 to 1906 and from 1914 to 1924, and as state Grange Lecturer from 1908 to 1914 and from 1930 to 1934, which was the year before she died. Buell also wrote a page of advice for Lecturers in the *National Grange Monthly*, compiled her ideas about Grange leadership into a substantial book, *The Grange Master and the Grange Lecturer* (1921), appeared at Lecturers' conferences all over the country, and spoke for the Grange before the Michigan State Federation of Women's Clubs and various gatherings of rural women in several states. A prolific essayist, she contributed to magazines such as the *American Garden*, the *American Agriculturist*, *Good Housekeeping*, and *The Woman's Magazine*.[44]

Her writings were highly colored by Swedenborgianism. One manuscript essay, written on Michigan State Grange letterhead in 1891, summarizes Swedenborg's doctrine of correspondences. The seer taught that "our surroundings in the life which is not mortal, will be, as it were, pictures of what is going on within us." Even in this mortal life, she continued, "the outward man, we well know, is but the impression of the inner." Thus, high ideals could shape the material world; people could give their ideals tangible form by improving livestock, plants, and everything else around them. Undertaken in that spirit, she believed, hard work was not drudgery but a thoroughly satisfying expression of the worker's lofty intentions. Work done out of doors, surrounded by the beauties of nature, was particularly satisfying. Gardening, for example, was an "intelligent acquaintanceship with vegetable structure" that was accessible to any thoughtful person, however well or poorly educated.[45]

Buell was more ambitiously philosophical than Mayo, Gifford, or any other prominent Grange women—except Bristol—ever chose to be. But she applied her lofty thoughts to the practical matters that also concerned most of them. She wanted to alleviate drudgery among farm women, both by helping them to understand their work and by urging them to use appliances "that will save the back and give the brain some leisure to itself." Concerned about women's health, she urged them to walk, drive horses on excursions away from their farms, and play tennis. If young people saw that such enjoyments were available on farms, she argued, they would stay in the country rather than running off to supposedly more interesting cities. Her practical interests also included educational opportunities for women and equal suffrage. She was one of two women who directed the Michigan State Grange campaign for an equal suffrage amendment to the state constitution in 1912.[46]

Much as Buell admired Mayo's example of devotion to farm and family, she chose to lead her own life very differently. Single and urban, resident for many years in Ann Arbor, she was one of several women who pursued independent careers that included Grange work. The Reverend Olivia Woodman was another. Woodman married, but only after she had lived for fifty years and found a calling to which she remained devoted for the rest of her life. Much the same can be said of Dora Stockman, who saw herself as the successor to Mayo, Woodman, and Buell among Michigan Grange women. She was a state Grange Lecturer for sixteen years, wrote books, and held elective offices. She farmed for a few years, married, and raised two children, but she also made a far more independent career than Mayo's responsibilities to family and farm allowed her to do.[47]

Other independent women came to prominence in various parts of the Grange at the end of the last century and the beginning of this one. Dr. Hannah McK. Lyons, for example, graduated from the Women's Medical College of Philadelphia in 1893, worked many years for the Inter-State Dairy Council, lectured about nutrition in the Philadelphia schools, and also served the Methodist Episcopal Church, the WCTU, and the Grange. Leader of the Pennsylvania State Grange home economics committee for ten years, Lyons regularly contributed articles about nutrition and home economics to state and national Grange publications. She married, but that does not seem to have impeded her medical and educational career.[48] Similarly, the Reverend Minnie Fenwick, First Lecturer of the Wyoming State Grange, which began in 1913, maintained an active ministry while also helping her husband and ministerial colleague to establish a farm and raise four children. Licensed by the Des Moines Christian Conference in 1888 and ordained in 1900, she started three preaching circuits around Burns, Wyoming, where she moved in 1907, founded Sunday schools, and helped to lead the WCTU, of which she was Wyoming state President for five years.[49]

One of Fenwick's western contemporaries, Agnes Ludwig Riddle, also combined marriage and farming with an extraordinary public life. Born in Silesia in 1865, Riddle came to the United States when she was sixteen, lived briefly in the east, and then moved to St. Louis, where she studied domestic science and nursing. She married Joseph Riddle, a dairy farmer, after she had begun to work in a Colorado hospital. Riddle taught Sunday school, preached in the neighborhood around her husband's farm, and became Secretary of the Colorado State Grange, a member of the advisory board of Colorado's agricultural college, and a Republican state Senator representing Adams, Arapahoe, and Elbert counties for one term after the 1911 election. She was the first woman legislator in Colorado and the first Grange woman elected to a legislature anywhere in the country. Particularly interested in rural education, she is credited with helping to win appropriations for a women's building at the agricultural college and for extension programs serving remote areas of the state.[50]

Riddle's legislative career, though it lasted only one term, was extraordinary. When she won her senate seat, women in most of the country could not yet vote. But her personal success had parallels throughout the Order. Grange women achieved various kinds of public leadership, and some twentieth-century sisters carved out notably independent careers. Riddle also shared Grange women's universal interest in rural education, especially women's education at the agricultural college, and matched some of her sisters' devotion to agriculture, often doing chores early in the morning before going into Denver for Senate meetings. Only her ethnic background and profession made Riddle truly unusual. Immigrants and nurses were rarities in the Grange; old stock Americans and teachers were typical.

When Riddle died in 1930, the *Denver Post* suggested a connection between her Grange service and her election to the senate. Being Secretary of the state Grange had made her "widely known, admired and trusted by the farmers."[51] Probably her religious activities had already given her some neighborhood celebrity, but the Grange made her a prominent person. Similarly, many other women leaders, notably Carr, Baird, and Mayo, were known mostly for their Grange activities; Howland, Kimball, Gifford, Buell, and Fenwick had other kinds of celebrity, but the Grange was an important outlet for all of their ambitions. It gave them, and many less conspicuous women, various measures of prominence.

Apart from their Grange activities and at least partially consequent fame, the leaders described here shared several interests and attributes. Typically high school or normal school graduates and often former teachers, they were devoted to education. Religious, in both mainline Protestant and unconventional ways, they worked for various kinds of spiritual and moral uplift. Finally, they all saw the Grange as an instrument for improving the status of women. They defined the necessary improvements differently, but they all thought that women were somehow stunted by the limitations that the conditions of rural life, male thoughtlessness, and their own unreflecting submission to custom had imposed on them. And they all thought that the Grange had a part to play in rural women's liberation.

NOTES

1. Hesterman, "The History of Edina," 14–15; Bertels, "The National Grange," 17; Gerald L. Prescott, "Wisconsin Farm Leaders in the Gilded Age," *Agricultural History* 44 (April 1970): 183–99; Lee Benson, *Merchants, Farmers and Railroads* (Cambridge: Harvard University Press, 1955); Carl Degler, *At Odds: Women and the Family in America from the Revolution to the Present* (New York: Oxford University Press, 1980), 322, 335.

2. Wagner, "Farms, Families, and Reform," 33.

3. *The Husbandman* 1 (23 June 1875): 2; *Grange Visitor* 11 (15 January 1885): 3. Probably Mayo's speech dealt with domestic relations, which was among her favorite subjects. Mayo disparaged classical learning for its own sake; all knowledge had to be justified by practical usefulness.

4. *National Grange* 5 (10 November 1909).

5. *Bulletin* 4 (May 1878); this is discussed in Chapter 1.

6. *Journal of Proceedings of the Fourteenth Annual Session of the Pennsylvania State Grange*, 1886, 32.

7. *Pennsylvania Grange News* 11 (November 1914): 97, 109; Kenyon Butterfield makes a great point of the Order's pervasive "religious spirit" in *Chapters in Rural Progress* (Chicago: University of Chicago Press, 1909), 159.

8. *Farmer's Friend and Grange Advocate* 19 (1 October 1892): 1; the Order's relations with Catholics, Lutherans, and conservative evangelicals are considered in this study's introduction.

9. *Bulletin* 4 (August 1878); David B. Tyack and Myra H. Strober, *Women and Men in the Schools: A History of the Sexual Structuring of Educational Employment* (Palo Alto: National Institute of Education, 1981), 10–11.

10. Hebb, "The Woman Movement in the California State Grange," 47.

11. *Farmer's Friend and Grange Advocate* 21 (17 November 1894): 1.

12. Carol Farley Kessler, *Daring to Dream: Utopian Stories By United States Women: 1836–1919* (Boston: Pandora Press, 1984), 95; Hayden, *The Grand Domestic Revolution*, 92.

13. Ray Reynolds, *Cat's Paw Utopia* (El Cajon, California: Ray Reynolds, 1972), 38.

14. Ibid., 38–39.

15. Marie Howland, "Biographical Sketch of Edward Howland," *The Credit Foncier of Sinaloa* 5 (1 March 1891): N.p.; Marie Howland, "The Patrons of Husbandry," *Lippincott's Magazine of Popular Literature and Science* 12 (September 1873): 342.

16. Howland, "The Patrons of Husbandry," 339; Howland, "Biographical Sketch of Edward Howland," N.p.; *Proceedings of the Second Annual Session of New Jersey State Grange*, 1875, 5, 16; Hayden, *The Grand Domestic Revolution*, 101.

17. Marie Howland, Hammonton, 19 January 1876, to William Saunders, in National Grange Records, Cornell University Library.

18. Frances E. Willard and Mary A. Livermore, eds., *A Woman of the Century* (Buffalo, Chicago, and New York: Charles Wells Moulton, 1893), 123–24; Bessie Bristol Mason, "Memories of My Mother, Augusta Cooper Bristol, 1835–1910," *The Vineland Historical Magazine* (July–October 1952): 42–48.

19. Nichols is one of few Grange women described in Edward T. James, Janet Wilson James, and Paul Boyer, eds., *Notable American Women 1607–1950* (Cambridge: Harvard University Press, 1971), 2: 625–27, though her Grange association is not mentioned there; Ida Husted Harper, *History of Woman Suffrage* (New York: Arno Press, 1969), 5: 247 reports that Dr. Anna Howard Shaw, a *Notable* of somewhat greater magnitude, was also a Grange member; Hebb, "The Woman Movement in the California State Grange," 47; *Pacific Rural Press* 21 (29 January 1881): 70.

20. "My Own Story," a manuscript fragment in several versions in the Jeanne C. Carr Papers, Huntington Library; Hebb, "The Woman Movement in the California State Grange," 105.

21. Hebb, "The Woman Movement in the California State Grange," 38, 93, 80, 50, 105.

22. *The Woman's Journal* 29 (23 July 1898): 237; Richard F. Pourade, *The History of San Diego* (San Diego: Union-Tribune Publishing Co., 1964), 4:30; Hebb, "The Woman Movement in the California State Grange," 39, 47–48.

23. "The Bread Winners of Briarfield," with many of Flora Kimball's other writings in scrapbooks held by the National City Public Library.

24. "Woman's Relationship to Society Through the Grange," an undated leaflet from the National Grange Lecture Department, in the National Agricultural Library, and also published in *The Husbandman* 14 (11 January 1888): 3.

25. Untitled speech in Gifford papers, Patterson Library and Art Gallery.

26. Leonard L. Allen, *History of the New York State Grange* (Watertown: The Grange, 1934), 63; *Centennial History of Chautauqua County* (Jamestown: The Chautauqua History Co., 1904), 2: 288–91; undated papers in Gifford manuscripts, Patterson Library and Art Gallery.

27. *The Westfield Republican* (24 August 1910).

28. *Representative Men and Old Families of Rhode Island: Genealogical Records and*

Historical Sketches of Prominent and Representative Citizens and of Many of the Old Families (Chicago: J. H. Beers and Co., 1908), 2:1254; Carpenter's pronouncements on temperance and suffrage will be discussed in Chapter 6.

29. *National Grange Monthly* 20 (5 May 1923): 2; *National Grange* 1 (4 March 1908): 8; Hesterman, "The History of Edina," 27; entry for January 23, 1886 in Sarah Baird diaries, Division of Archives and Manuscripts, Minnesota Historical Society; *Minneapolis Journal* 3 and 6 (April 1923).

30. Hesterman, "The History of Edina," 16–26; "Minnehaha Spray" manuscript in Minnehaha Grange No. 398 Papers, Division of Archives and Manuscripts, Minnesota Historical Society.

31. Hesterman, "The History of Edina," 11, 45; *National Grange Monthly* 20 (May 1923): 2; *Proceedings of the Minnesota State Grange, Twenty-Fourth Annual Session, 1892* (Minneapolis: State Grange, 1893), 15–16.

32. Mayo is remembered in her friend Jennie Buell's *One Woman's Work For Farm Women*, which is the principal source for information about her life, and in Claribel R. Barnett, "Mayo, Mary Anne Bryant," *Dictionary of American Biography* (New York: Charles Scribner's Sons, 1933), 6: 462–63; Liberty Hyde Bailey, *Cyclopedia of American Agriculture* (New York: The Macmillan Co., 1909), 4: 594; *Biographical Review of Calhoun County, Michigan* (Chicago: Hobart and Mather, 1904), 427; James Bryant, "More Than Hard Work and Good Butter," *Michigan History* 65 (July/August, 1981): 32–36; Donald B. Marti, "Woman's Work in the Grange: Mary Ann Mayo of Michigan, 1882–1903," *Agricultural History* 56 (April 1982): 439–52.

33. Buell, *One Woman's Work*, 3–7; Robert S. Mayo, unpublished notes on his grandmother, made available by Mr. Mayo.

34. Buell, *One Woman's Work*, 9–10.

35. Ibid., 12; *Biographical Review of Calhoun County*, 426; Joseph E. Gould, *The Chautauqua Movement* (Albany: State University of New York Press, 1961), 3–10; Jennie Buell, Schoolcraft, to Mary Mayo, 8 January 1886, Mary Mayo letters, Michigan State University Archives and Historical Collections.

36. Buell, *One Woman's Work*, 10; *Grange Visitor* 8 (1 August 1882): 6.

37. *Grange Visitor* 6 (1 November 1880): 6.

38. *Sixteenth Annual Report of the Secretary of the State Board of Agriculture of the State of Michigan* (Lansing: The State, 1878), 132–34.

39. *Nineteenth Annual Report of the Secretary of the State Board of Agriculture of the State of Michigan*, 1880, 1934–96.

40. Buell, *One Woman's Work*, 23.

41. Ibid., 24–25; *Grange Visitor* 10 (15 March 1884): 6; (1 July 1884): 6.

42. *Grange Visitor* 11 (1 October 1886): 1.

43. Catherine F. Hitching, "Universalist and Unitarian Women Ministers," *The Journal of the Universalist Historical Society* 10 (1975): 155; *National Grange Monthly* 10 (May 1913): 8; John William Leonard, *Woman's Who's Who of America* (New York: Commonwealth Co., 1914), 901; John William Leonard, *The Grange in Michigan: An Agricultural History of Michigan Over the Past Ninety Years* (Grand Rapids: Fred Trump, 1963), 49.

44. Leonard, *Woman's Who's Who of America*, 143; *National Grange Monthly* 8 (October 1911): 7; 24 (May 1927): 1; notes on Michigan Grange women in Cyrus H. Jasperce Papers, Michigan Historical Collection, Bentley Historical Library,

University of Michigan; clippings of Buell's publications in Barber Buell Papers, Michigan Historical Collection.

45. Clippings and manuscript in the Barber Buell Papers, Michigan Historical Collection.

46. Clippings, especially "A Breezy Word from Michigan" from the *American Agriculturist* (June 1890), in the Barber Buell Papers, Michigan Historical Collection; Buell's role in the 1912 suffrage campaign is described in Chapter 6.

47. Stockman will be described more fully in Chapter 7.

48. *National Grange* 5 (10 April 1910): 6; *Penn State Alumni News* 18 (February 1932): 6; *Daily Local News* (Westchester, Pennsylvania), 7 May 1946.

49. "Minnie and Cyrus Fenwick, Pioneer Ministers of Burns," a typescript in the Wyoming State Historical Research and Publication Division; Mrs. Alfred H. Beach, *Women of Wyoming* (Casper: S. & E. Boyer Co., 1927), 1: 533–35; *National Grange Monthly* 14 (February 1917): 14.

50. *National Grange Monthly* 8 (August 1911): 9; *Denver Post* 5 (May 1930).

51. *Denver Post* 5 (May 1930).

3

Literary Entertainment

In 1888, Flora Kimball observed that "from one end of our grand republic to the other the pen of the farmers' wives and daughters is busy." Women were bringing "timely words of wisdom" to Grange meetings, exercising their influence "in the cause of temperance and moral reform," and proving themselves peers of the "highest lady of the land." Kimball guessed that the Grange had awakened the "slumbering genius of a hundred thousand women."[1] Twenty years later, Mortimer Whitehead, a National Grange Lecturer who consistently emphasized women's part in Grange work, repeated the same thought and many of Kimball's words. He guessed that "hundreds of thousands of women" had found occasions to speak and write in the Grange.[2]

Neither Flora Kimball nor Mortimer Whitehead actually counted the women who contributed to the Order's discussions and literature, but certainly a great many otherwise obscure women had found their voices in the Order. In 1876, for example, "M" told readers of the *Dirigo Rural*, Maine's Grange journal, that previously silent women were writing essays, making speeches, and surprising both themselves and the "Lords of Creation" with their talent.[3] And two years later, a contributor to the "Sisters' Column" of the Wisconsin State Grange *Bulletin* observed that "sisters who two or three years ago could not stand before their neighbors and friends and say half a dozen words, have from small and feeble beginnings developed into easy and graceful speakers."[4] That development came hard. In 1898, a woman told her Ohio Pomona Grange that the farmers' wives who first spoke before Granges, Farmers' Institutes, and Alliances began with "infantile weakness and modesty." But that "was before women had discovered themselves!" The Grange, she claimed, had been among the principal means of that discovery.[5]

Grange women's speeches, letters, essays, and occasional stories and poems are remarkable for their uniformity. For at least half a century, starting in the 1870s, women writers treated much the same themes in much the same ways. Their emphases varied, and they sometimes disagreed about whether women should vote and if pie-making was a waste of time, but, with few exceptions, the sisters argued within a fairly narrow range of opinions that varied remarkably little from place to place and over time. Their writing, with a few exceptions, records settled, widely shared beliefs, not controversy and development.

Grangers found most of their opportunities to speak in local, or subordinate, meetings. Subordinate Granges typically met every two weeks, which meant that a lot of programs had to be filled with discussion and literature. Selections from books and magazines and declamations of famous speeches met part of the need, but Grangers also liked to hear each others' original words. Local Granges did not usually preserve texts or detailed summaries of members' contributions, but their records show that discussions, essays, and poems were common and that women contributed their full share. A Pennsylvania sister guessed that women were less active in discussion than men but thought that they presented just as many essays, poems, and other creations that could be prepared in advance. Grange minutes and other reports of meetings confirm at least the second part of her impression.[6]

Some contributions to local Grange programs have been preserved. For example, Minneihaha Grange No. 398, just west of Minneapolis, recorded some of its programs in substantial detail and, at the end of its first year, in December 1874, collected several members' essays into a sort of magazine called "The Minnehaha Spray." Sarah Baird, later Master of the Minnesota State Grange, assembled the "Spray" and read it to a meeting. Its unifying theme was the need for cultural self-improvement among farmers. One anonymous contributor expressed deep resentment of city people's disrespect for agriculture and hoped that higher intellectual attainments in the country might improve farmers' social standing.[7] Later, in 1879, Minnehaha Grange began to appoint three-member committees to plan "Literary entertainment." The first program under that system was an original comic play that was successful enough to encourage another theatrical effort entitled "Female Suffering." In the 1880s, Minnehaha Grange literary committees assigned members to present selections, music, and original essays. One fairly typical 1883 meeting featured a song performed by a brother, selections recited by various sisters, and a sister's original essay on the "economy of practical house keeping on the farm." The assignment system spread literary responsibility widely, especially among the sisters.[8]

Hastings Grange in New York at first left literary work mostly to its Lecturer. Rosie Strickland, who held the office in 1875, personally contributed essays, poems, and selections. Her successor, Sister Wadsworth, also read selections and an account of her visit to another Grange but tried to get other members involved in programs. Topics for discussion at one meeting included grafting fruit trees and "What is the best way to cook potatoes?" That provided something for all of the members, orchardists and cooks, men and women.[9] Another New York subordinate assured that balance in 1875 by choosing a committee of three sisters and two brothers to devise entertainments and propose discussion topics. Their first program featured a discussion of breadmaking led by two sisters, readings by a brother and a sister, and a discussion of fall seeding led by two brothers. Perhaps not quite satisfied with the result, they planned a discussion for the next meeting on how to make their programs more interesting.[10]

Other New York Granges found distinctive ways to get women involved in their programs. In 1876, Chemung Valley Grange conducted a series of discussions on housekeeping and sent detailed reports, with texts of some speeches, to *The Husbandman*, New York's Grange journal. The discussions went well, a member observed, after participants learned to address the whole group, rather than conversing with the people seated nearest. The Chemung brothers listened quietly; some of them were surprised that "the ladies were so ready in debate."[11] Other women, who were less ready to speak up, needed help and encouragement. For example, "Mern" of Delphi Grange, who was probably its Lecturer, got each of her more retiring sisters to write a few lines about "Home," which she pieced together as a kind of homiletic quilt. It said that home was "the dearest spot in the world," a refuge from the world's cares, and the scene of childhood joys. After its successful presentation to Delphi Grange, the essay appeared in *The Husbandman*. The sisters produced another patchwork essay, on temperance, soon after that.[12]

Not all Granges were so careful to give women an equal share in their programs. In 1874, for example, the brothers of Kendaia Grange No. 64 in Seneca County, New York, focused their discussions on wheat growing and the costs of threshing various grains. Women participated very little, though brothers gratefully accepted their offer to sew regalia. Minutes of later Kendaia Grange meetings, for the years from 1886 to 1892, show the sisters taking a far more active part.[13] That tendency may have been general; some Granges increased their efforts to involve women after the Order's early boom years ended.[14] But there were exceptions. The sisters of Olive Grange No. 189 in eastern Indiana were as silent in the late 1880s and early 1890s as the Kendaia women had been in 1874. They joined, served in the women's offices, and heard discussions that almost always concerned crops. If any woman took a leading part in those discussions, secretaries failed to notice.[15]

Although Grange women met with less than universal encouragement, sisters all over the country contributed to discussions and presented papers through the whole period of this study. For example, a historian of the early southern Granges reports that their meetings included literary work and that women contributed essays on topics such as "Beautifying the Home" and preserving fruit.[16] A Mississippi woman, though protesting that she had no time to write, honored her Lecturer's request for an essay by reflecting on women's hard work, the wisdom of taking time for intellectual pleasures such as writing for the Grange, and the difficulty of teaching children good morals where they had so much contact with African-Americans.[17] Midwestern women, also concerned about morality and housework, entertained meetings with talks about "The Christian Voter," labor-saving appliances, and other lofty and practical topics.[18] And a Delaware Grange, which had emphasized cooperative buying to the apparent exclusion of educational programs through its first six years, called upon women to set a new direction in 1880. Ceres and Pomona, who were assigned to write papers "on enlightening subjects," responded so enthusiastically that their program had to be continued to a second meeting.[19] Particularly ambitious contributions to local Grange meetings all over the country appeared in the *National Grange* magazine early in this century. It carried a Colorado Lecturer's thoughts on educating country girls, a Minnesota sister's paper on the benefits of raising flowers, and a Massachusetts paper on the moral importance of home. Their authors, like many women who contributed to Grange literature, were eager to show that they had read great books. The Minnesota and Massachusetts women both quoted Ruskin in support of their arguments.[20]

The Grange also provided some important forums above the subordinate level. Pomona Granges, which were drawn from the membership of subordinate Granges throughout entire counties, typically met once a month for ritual and business in the morning, dinner at noon, and educational programs in the afternoon. If attendance at afternoon sessions was especially heavy, they might move from the host Grange's hall to a nearby church. Programs were proportionately ambitious. In 1881, when Mary Mayo reported to Michigan's Grange journal as secretary of the Calhoun County Pomona, she described a September session that included several discussions and essays. Perry Mayo led the meeting's consideration of the changes "necessary in legislation and business methods, to enable laborers and producers to retain in their hands an equitable proportion of the results of their own labor." He attacked monopolies and legislation that favored particular classes. Then a sister presented an essay on the history of printing, and other women led discussions of the vexed Russian situation, butter pricing, and whether enough United States history was taught in schools. (The Calhoun County Grangers quickly agreed that their children were learning enough of the national history.)[21] Similarly, the Hennepin County, Minnesota, Pomona held an 1881 meeting that started with a closed business session, progressed through a lavish dinner, and concluded with an open afternoon meeting that featured original essays on the Grange by two sisters, readings of "The Edina Spray" and a similar production from the Bloomington Grange, vocal and instrumental music by some of the younger sisters, and selections recited by Grange children.[22] The Loraine County, Ohio, Pomona varied the usual pattern in 1897 when several women presented essays and recitations in the morning, "Bros. Crocker and Adams" served a "bountiful dinner," and the Grange met for business that afternoon. Sister Crocker presented an original, perhaps extraordinarily authoritative, essay on "Woman's influence in the country home."[23]

Women also presented papers and led discussions at state Grange meetings, at gatherings of women held in connection with state Grange meetings, and on other especially important occasions. In 1875, Jeanne Carr started a series of meetings for women members of the California State Grange; participants, especially Carr herself, considered dress reform, equal suffrage, and other topics of special interest to them. A Pennsylvania sister orated to her state Grange in 1885 about the deficiencies of farm homes, and the Ohio State Grange of 1892 assigned a woman to read a paper on what the Grange had done for women. Perhaps the most original performance of that kind was a sort of science fiction story, anticipating Edward Bellamy's *Looking Backward*, presented by a woman member of the Missouri State Grange in 1887. It described a 1900 trip in an airship that a Granger had invented and given to the Order. Grange aviation had forced the railroads to operate honestly. It had also made the Order powerful; the President of the United States in 1900 had been Master of the Missouri State Grange in 1887. The speeches and essays read in such statewide forums were clearly star performances, not ordinary Grange papers, as were the speeches given at major Grange picnics.[24]

Picnics were favorite Grange entertainments that often featured oratory by well-known Grange leaders, including some women. The best known of the picnics was the big event that the Pennsylvania State Grange held at Williams Grove every year from 1873 to 1916. It started as a perfectly ordinary one-day picnic, stretched to three days in 1879, and took an entire week after a few more years. At its height, the picnic drew approximately 150,000 people from as many as twenty-nine states. Attractions included livestock, farm implements, appliances such as sewing machines, and oratory by Grange leaders and politicians.[25]

Women produced some of the oratory starting in 1890, when the woman's work committee of the Pennsylvania State Grange staged a one-hour program on making "Woman's work more effective for the 'Good of the Order.' " One year later, the picnic managers erected a tent, with seats for several hundred people, in which the sisters could have all the meetings they wanted without, as the chairman of the woman's work committee understood their purposes, "infringing upon the brothers' political discussions, or settlement of the vexed tax question." Whatever the managers' intentions may have been, the women's meeting became an extraordinary opportunity for women orators.[26]

The 1891 woman's work program at Williams Grove started with a report by the committee chairman, as her title was, and a speech by Eliza Gifford of New York. Gifford answered questions about the woman's work committee in her state and then probably talked about equal suffrage, which was always her favorite subject. The program, which took several days, also included music, which men came to hear, reports from woman's work committees in subordinate Granges, two speeches by Carrie Twing, a well-known Grange orator from New York, and essays read by Pennsylvania sisters. One of the essays argued that men and women should behave as equals without losing sight of their differences; another surveyed women's progress in Grange offices. The Grange doctrine of equality, the second concluded, was gaining practical significance.[27]

Picnickers heard about woman's work again in 1892. Elizabeth Lord, yet another visiting orator from the New York State Grange, and the Reverend Anna Shaw, a famous suffragist, addressed meetings of suffrage and temperance advocates. The Pennsylvania State Grange woman's work committee also arranged to have several sisters read papers on the Order's educational benefits and the need for women to realize that they must help to elevate society "to a purer and better standard." One paper suggested that farm women would not have been likely to take a summer week for intellectual and social enjoyments twenty-five years earlier; the fact that some women were doing exactly that at Williams Grove was a measure of what the Order had accomplished. The paper went on to express sympathy with the Homestead strikers while criticizing their methods. Another woman took much the same line about the strikers, adding that the Populist movement offered hope of economic reform. She thought that helping to "wrest the government of this country from the . . . monopolistic power that now holds it" was a legitimate part of woman's work, and she also opined that Philadelphia and Pittsburgh got too much of the state's school fund, girls should not wear corsets before the age of twenty, the Pope's foreign minions were a danger to America, boys should not smoke, and Edward Bellamy's *Looking Backward* was an instructive book.[28]

The Williams Grove picnic was an important women's forum through most of the 1890s. After 1898, however, picnic reports in the *Farmer's Friend and Grange Advocate*, which was the official organ of the Pennsylvania State Grange, had little to say about women's participation. Their programs ended, apparently, when the state Grange discontinued its committee on woman's work; the Pennsylvania Ceres complained that the committee's demise had curtailed women's activity.[29] Whatever killed its women's programs, the picnic was important to Grange women only briefly. The *Farmer's Friend*, which published women's picnic speeches, served them far more consistently. Most strong Grange states had something like Pennsylvania's journal, and most of those publications actively sought women's contributions. Sometimes their desire for material to fill women's columns was greater than the sisters' readiness to contribute. Editors and interested women frequently exhorted laggard writers to do their duty.[30]

Grange women gave the journals reports of meetings, papers and poems that they had read in their neighborhood subordinate Granges or in the grander meetings of county Pomona Granges, occasional stories, and a great many letters. They directed most of their contributions to the "Ladies' Department," "Sisters' Column," or "Household Economy" sections; Grange journals nearly always had such features, which emphasized, but were not limited to, domestic crafts, and they were effectively reserved for women. After "Bach," presumably a male correspondent, offered a few thoughts on cooking and housekeeping to New York's Grange journal, "Letta" guessed that he had learned the domestic arts from his mother and judged that "boys who follow their mothers around with needle and thread are not generally the stuff of which our staunch men are made." A Michigan woman—Grange journals circulated beyond their own states—promptly defended male interest in such matters, and another man defiantly sent his recipe for mince pie, but "Letta" had surely expressed the orthodox view. The women's departments of Grange journals were for women almost exclusively.[31]

Most contributors wrote briefly, as did someone who told the Wisconsin State Grange *Bulletin* that she felt obliged to send a few words even though "writing is hard work for me." So she described her subordinate Grange, which was not flourishing, and asked other women to write their thoughts about butter making and chicken raising.[32] Similarly, "Lovica" wrote a few lines about her farm work to New York's *Husbandman*. She milked, made cheese, and did other farm work, too, because her husband was a "little fellow" and had no hired hand.[33] Neither "Lovica" nor the Wisconsin sister had much leisure for writing, but they valued the opportunities that Grange journals provided to say something about their experience and make contact with similar women.

Other women wrote far more. Famous names such as Flora Kimball, Mary Mayo, and Eliza Gifford appeared in the journals regularly and sometimes at great length. Flora Kimball, who frequently wrote for California Grange publications, occupied five closely printed columns in the *California Patron* with her story, "The Bread Winner of Briarfield."[34] Other prolific contributors never attained such fame because they were known to their readers only by pseudonyms. One woman, who gave her name, complained that too much of what appeared in the "Ladies' Department" of Michigan's *Grange Visitor* was signed "Aunt Margaret," "Myra," or "Betsey." Observing that men never used pen names, she urged women to be just as forthright. Then "Aunt Margaret," who called herself Mrs. M. J. Spencer for the occasion, explained that pen names reflected "the modesty that pervades a woman's mind."[35] Such modest women occasionally let their ordinary names slip into print, but most of them forfeited literary recognition.

Women's contributions to Grange journals and meetings focused on a few topics. Occasionally, women asserted that they were interested in everything that men were and wrote about economics and farm operations, but that was highly unusual. Southern Grange leaders observed that women stayed away from discussions of cooperatives but were just as reliably attracted to any program about children. Similarly, Mary Mayo noticed that "every man" had ideas about great public questions such as tariffs, and "we women like to listen and occasionally take a hand," but too much concentration on public and agricultural issues discouraged women's participation. Women should take a full share in Grange discussions, Mayo insisted, which meant that some discussion topics should be chosen especially for them; she suggested home sanitation and whether women should learn about farming.[36] A Pennsylvania woman later made similar suggestions. She had tried to recruit a farm woman who refused to join because Grange discussions always concerned agriculture, in which she had no interest. The Grange woman thought that was foolish; women should understand farming if only so that they could fend for themselves if left alone. But she recognized that women preferred to talk about "home keeping, housekeeping, cooking, music, literature, history," and public matters such as the war between Japan and Russia. Women could not vote, but they liked to be kept informed about the world so that they could "help our voters to vote."[37]

In fact, women did have their own preferred topics that had to be included in Grange programs to keep the sisters interested. Accordingly, the Maryland State Grange committee on the good of the Order admonished brothers in 1898 that both men and women should take women's subjects seriously.[38] The most popular of those subjects were housekeeping, cooking, child rearing, and the blessings that the Grange conferred upon women. Much as they resembled their contemporaries in womens' study clubs in their determination to foster each others' intellectual and rhetorical ambition, Grangers differed from club women in their emphasis on practical, domestic topics.[39]

Grangers had a consistent and thoroughly conventional view of domesticity. A Michigan sister summarized it precisely in an 1880 talk to her Grange, stating that "the wife's true sphere is the family." It encompassed "domestic duties which custom has assigned her" and a higher responsibility to "polish and refine the characters of those with whom she associates." The speaker then expressed measured support for equal suffrage because women's "purifying, refining, ennobling" influence should extend into public life.[40] Similarly, a Massachusetts woman told her Grange in 1909 that home was a dignified and rewarding field of endeavor that extended much beyond individual households. One of the glories of Christian civilization, she argued, was the importance that it attached to domesticity and, therefore, to women.[41]

The domestic sphere included much more than housework and cooking. But it necessarily started with those chores. "Floy" told fellow New York Grangers that even women who had servants should become expert housekeepers; to ignore the art was "an outrage against womanly nature."[42] Grangers also believed that women needed expertise so that they could do housework efficiently and save time for their higher functions. Grange women, therefore, used much of their space in publications and time on programs to exchange household hints that displayed their skills and promised to make other women more efficient. Use ammonia instead of soap to wash windows; make dusters out of turkey feathers; cover kitchen shelves with paper; store flour in lard cans; put springs on kitchen doors to keep them shut and flies out.[43] And more than all of that, they told each other, cook well. Cooking, as competitions at agricultural fairs routinely demonstrated, was a much respected art. Grange women displayed their mastery by serving meals at Grange meetings and discussing particular techniques and recipes.

Occasionally, women complained that their sisters lavished too much attention on cookery. In 1878, for example, "Alice" protested that the "Ladies' Department" of the *Indiana Farmer* was "almost filled with cake recipes." She was especially dismayed that a woman had sent, and the *Farmer* had printed, a recipe using wine; "there is so much need for every lady to be using her influence in every way for temperance."[44] Another Indiana sister criticized overemphasis on cooking less severely. She urged women to "prove that we have some thoughts beyond the kitchen and parlor, although it is true that the affairs of the kitchen are very important, and that this part of a lady's education should not be neglected."[45] "Filbert," who regularly contributed to New York's *Husbandman*, also called for balance soon after sending recipes for cake and lemon pie.[46]

The way to achieve balance, Grange women regularly suggested, was by simplifying meals and their preparation. For example, members of Chemung Valley Grange in New York called for simplicity throughout their wide-ranging series of discussions on cooking and housekeeping. In the matter of breakfast, one woman said that she did "not think that a great variety of dishes is necessary; a good cup of coffee with cream and sugar, broiled beef steak or fried ham and potatoes with bread, rolls or cakes, constitute what I believe to be a good breakfast." She also simplified preparation by boiling some extra potatoes the day before, rather than cooking her entire breakfast from scratch.[47] In the same spirit, Mary Mayo urged women to serve fresh apples instead of making cider, "which is only fit for vinegar," or combining fruit with "time, toil, and lard" to make pie.[48] Pie was a favorite example of rural excess. "Aunt Patience" called for a complete end to pastry cooking. If people concluded their meals with fruit and cheese, cookery could "retire, at least to the middle distance," making room in the foreground of women's lives for "mental culture and pleasant friendly social life."[49]

Women's greatest domestic responsibility, by common consent, was child-rearing. One New York sister called it "the highest function of the female life." In "the perfectly organized human female," motherhood was the "product of love founded upon reason and religion." It was all spiritual and intellectual.[50] It was also a heavy responsibility that women bore, judging from what Grange women typically said, with little help from men. An Ohio woman made that exceptionally explicit when she told her Pomona Grange that women could teach their children to be considerate and peaceful by stressing kindness to animals. Then she reflected that men were poor examples of kindness. The farm men she knew had "so many cruel things to do" and did them more brutally than necessary. She had seen frightened calves, feet trussed, heaped together in a wagon, bound for slaughter. Men did such things and were coarsened by them; women had to counteract their influence.[51] But a few Grange women objected to the common view that all good lessons were learned from mothers. A Wisconsin sister told her Grange that fathers shared responsibility for educating their daughters, and a woman who participated in the Chemung Valley, New York, discussions said that "the prevailing habit of exalting women serves to blind" men to their parental duties. But despite those exceptional comments, the "prevailing habit" was strong in the Grange, as it was among nineteenth-century, middle-class Americans generally.[52] When a Maine sister, writing from the authority of her forty-six terms of teaching, told her Grange that teachers needed cooperation from their students' homes, she laid the responsibility for that squarely on mothers, not parents.[53]

Grange writing about children started from the premise that they were a great blessing. Mary Mayo, who raised two, made that point in several stories that she contributed to the "Ladies' Department" of Michigan's *Grange Visitor*. One concerned the "loveless union" of two aging people who had no children. "The wife had married for a home, but her ideal home had never been realized." As the unsatisfying years went by, she abandoned her early efforts to "grace and adorn" her house and settled into a dull, pointless routine. Her husband, who "married because he thought that he could get more money with a wife, than without," was content in his miserly way. Then a dying mother left her baby in their care. In "their love for the baby, they began to love each other." Flowers "bloomed in the hitherto neglected yard, and the fragrant flowers of love bloomed in their hearts also." Then, when the baby was as "tall as the royal tiger lillys that blossomed in their door . . . God took their baby to himself." Sad as that was, the baby had permanently transformed the old people's lives.[54]

Mayo thought that children were essential to domestic happiness. She reiterated the point in a *Grange Visitor* piece that inferred domestic relations from small details that passersby could glimpse through the windows of various houses. Good homes appeared clean, but not rigidly ordered; they were full of cheerful, even slightly untidy, signs of children's presence. Books were left on tables, children played with brooms, carefully putting them away afterward, and women stopped cleaning in order to talk with children or read something to them. The details that made a home look warm and happy represented loving relations between children and their mothers.[55]

Grange women said that children should be treated with "gentleness, patience, calmness, firmness," and constant regard for their intellectual and moral development. A New Yorker urged her sisters to be sure that children always had plenty of good reading. Similarly, one of Mary Mayo's earliest contributions to the *Grange Visitor* warned that farm boys were likely to read "sensational, blood and thunder trash" unless their mothers saw that they got something wholesome. Girls were less drawn to improper literature, but all children would profit from seeing their mothers read edifying books. The maternal example, Mayo and a great many others insisted, was powerful.[56]

Grange women expressed a special concern about their daughters. Sons might be more apt to go astray morally, but intellectual neglect menaced farm girls. A Pennsylvania sister told her county Grange that farm people took their daughters out of school far too early because they thought that girls needed less education than boys did. Moreover, too many farm families made girls do field work rather than learning the household skills that they really needed. This particular abuse, she thought, was diminishing; presumably, her fellow Grangers had learned

better, but it was still a real problem among unprogressive farmers. Farm
people had to learn that girls needed education for the lofty sphere that
they would occupy as women.[57]

Girls learned their domestic calling from their mothers, chiefly, although Grangers also supported "domestic science" or "home economics" programs in schools and agricultural colleges.[58] Mothers taught
daughters by sharing work. "Aunt Ruth," a contributor to the "Sisters'
Column" of the Wisconsin State Grange *Bulletin,* made this point when
she criticized another woman for working hard while her daughters
relaxed. Because that woman was failing in a basic responsibility, her
daughters would grow up to be useless.[59] But other women suggested
that work had to be shared cautiously; if girls were forced to do housework, they would hate it for the rest of their lives. A New Yorker told
her Grange that girls should be persuaded to value housework as "ful-
filling a part of God's law."[60] A Michigan sister, taking the logic of that
much further, argued that girls deserved "an equal right" with boys to
choose their work. If they hated housework, they should attend school,
work in a shop, or do whatever they really wanted. No girl should work
unwillingly at home while waiting "for some man to come and marry
her" so that she could work in his home.[61] Similarly, an Ohio sister told
her Grange that girls should learn housekeeping but not that "their only
aim in life is to get married." At the beginning of the twentieth century,
she thought, most single women were as happy as those who married.[62]

More orthodox Grange women were anxious to keep their children
on the farm and their daughters properly domestic. They wanted their
daughters to work beside them, learn their skills, and live much as they
did. But they also wanted the girls to learn something more than ancient,
domestic crafts. The women who spoke and wrote for the Grange tried
to combine their hard work with intellectual pleasures, and they wanted
their daughters to excel them in that. They also resented the widespread
belief that ignorance befit girls who were going to spend their lives on
farms. A Wisconsin sister told her Grange in 1876 that farm girls had
as much need for general education "as the daughters of those of the
trades, and the professions, or of the millionaire." It would "lighten
labor and make home bright" as much for farm girls as for their counterparts in other social groups. Certainly, mathematics "will not make
them less efficient in butter-making, nor the classics in preparing the
chicken pie."[63] Much later, a Colorado sister argued that farm girls actually needed more education than did other young women; it helped
them to understand the advantages of rural life, which were not always
obvious to untutored minds. Lacking education, girls were apt to get
bored and want to move to town. They did not need college degrees,
or even high school diplomas, but they certainly required enough ed-

ucation to awaken their minds to the beauties of country life and prepare them to create refined homes and families.[64]

Arguing that young farm women needed education was part of Grangers' response to the canard that farming and ignorance naturally went together. Mary Mayo confronted that prejudice when a high school acquaintance expressed regret that Mayo had married a farmer and would probably lose the value of her education.[65] And a New York woman told her Grange that she had heard a town lady say that farm people "know nothing but of calves, pigs, and chicken."[66] Like other people who tried to speak for agriculture throughout its American history, Grangers resented being looked down upon. A Michigan sister put that resentment into a poem, "Only a Farmer's Daughter," which she contributed to her state's Grange journal.

> She is only a farmer's daughter,
>   A stylish lady said,
> With a scornful glance of her handsome eyes,
>   And a toss of her haughty head.
> Her hands, that sparkled with many a ring,
>   As fair as the lilly in hue
> They play the piano with wonderful grace—
>   'Tis the only work they do'.

The "stylish lady" was an uncharitable, thoroughly useless, ornament. By contrast, the poem went on to show, the despised farmer's daughter had wholesome, natural beauty, did useful work, and also played the piano. She had refinement and solid merit as well. She showed how really superior rural femininity could be if allowed to reach its full potential.[67]

The Grange, women routinely enthused, helped them to achieve that potential. The Reverend Aaron Grosh, first Chaplain of the National Grange, formulated the basic argument: that the Grange gave women respite from their confining labors, recognized their abilities, and broadened the range of their uplifting influence.[68] And generations of Grange women, all over the country, repeated each of his points with absolute fidelity. One very typical sister told her Indiana Grange that the Order had invited the farm woman "to lay aside her household cares, and bid a short adieu to the kitchen, and join her sisters and brothers, her neighbors and friends, in song and friendly greeting."[69] A Californian, in a similar speech to her Grange, said that she had lived on her ranch for twenty-five years before she joined the Order; she had never gotten to know any other women nor entertained any new thoughts. But then the Grange came to broaden her horizons. It gave her acquaintances from Shasta to San Diego along with important ideas about everything from making raisins to getting hens to set where she wanted them.[70] Occasionally, women objected that such grateful praise of the Order was overdone; in 1880, a weary sister asked if there was "any limit fixed to the time" for saying that the Grange had generously "*allowed*" women to join and had thereby started them on the way to better lives. The Grange really was a "long and important step for women," she wrote, but its praise had grown too fulsome for her taste.[71] Her complaint was exceptional. Women's tributes to the Order were typically unrestrained.

Perhaps the most complete summation of the Order's blessings to women was an essay that an anonymous sister contributed to *Country Gentleman*, one of the most durable and widely circulated farm magazines, in 1917. The author reported that she had grown up on a farm, attended the local schools, and then enrolled in a "rather select boarding school" in or near Boston where she enjoyed two years of "carefree, sheltered life." Forced to go home, she missed her city friends and city entertainments. She was bored, contemptuous of her rustic neighbors, and unreceptive to a stalwart young farmer who "tried to pay some attention" to her. She was determined not to marry a farmer, especially not one whose education had stopped at the local high school. Then a friend invited her to a Grange musical evening, caught measles just before the event, and left the unhappy young women to substitute for her at the piano. The meeting came as a revelation. The neighborhood Grangers enjoyed each others' society, and some of the sisters had more "grace and ease" than the young woman had expected of them. She came to respect her neighbors and to appreciate the satisfying possibilities of farm life, resumed her studies in order to participate intelligently in Grange discussions, overcame her shyness by reading a paper at a meeting, acquired useful new ideas about housekeeping, and thought of ways to improve her parents' home which her mother had allowed to fall behind her husband's progressive farm. Freshly inspired, mother and daughter remodeled their house with advice from home economists in the state agricultural college extension service. Then the young woman married her attentive farmer, whose merits she had learned to appreciate.[72]

The *Country Gentleman* story perfectly illustrates some of Grange women's favorite themes. Beginning with youthful discontent, a common worry among mothers who feared that their children would flee to the cities, it demonstrates that rural life, enlivened and dignified by the Grange, could be richly satisfying. It also affirms women's distinctive responsibilities, which could be illuminated by the science of home economics. It might have been constructed by Jennie Buell or some other expert as an epitome of the wisdom that Grange women had constantly and consistently shared with each other since the Order was new.[73]

NOTES

1. Flora Kimball, "Woman's Relation to Society Through the Grange," undated circular from National Grange Lecture Department, in National Agricultural Library, also *The Husbandman* 14 (11 January 1888): 3.

2. *National Grange* 2 (27 May 1908): 4.

3. *Dirigo Rural* 3 (17 June 1876): 3.

4. *Bulletin* 4 (May 1878).

5. *American Grange Bulletin and Scientific Farmer* 24 (27 October 1898): 10–11.

6. *Farmer's Friend and Grange Advocate* 18 (10 October 1891): 5.

7. "Minnehaha Spray" in papers of Minnehaha Grange No. 398, Archives and Manuscripts Division, Minnesota Historical Society.

8. Minutes of Minnehaha Grange No. 398 for 19 December 1879, 16 January 1880, and 19 May 1883 in papers of Minnehaha Grange No. 398, Archives and Manuscripts Division, Minnesota Historical Society.

9. Minutes of Hastings Grange No. 339 for 22 December 1875, 1 March 1876, and 15 December 1876 in New York State Grange Records, Cornell University Library.

10. Minutes of Clymer Grange for 11 and 25 September 1875 in New York State Grange Records, Cornell University Library.

11. *The Husbandman* 3 (22 November 1876): 2.

12. Ibid. 12 (3 March 1886): 2; (12 May 1886): 2.

13. Minutes of Kendaia Grange No. 64, entries for 1874 and for the years from 1886 through 1892, in New York Grange Records, Cornell University Library.

14. Hebb, "The Woman Movement in the California State Grange," 62; Smith, "The History of the Iowa State Grange," 5–6.

15. Minutes of Olive Grange No. 189 in the Indiana Historical Society.

16. Calvert, "The Southern Grange," 152–53.

17. *American Grange Bulletin and Scientific Farmer* 21 (3 September 1896): 10–11.

18. Ibid. 24 (27 October 1908): 12; 4 (16 August 1909): 15.

19. Carpenter, "History of Centre Grange From 1874 to 1949," 5.

20. *National Grange* 2 (15 July 1908): 12; 3 (28 April 1909): 12; 4 (19 May 1909): 12.

21. Gardner, *The Grange*, 358–59; *Grange Visitor* 7 (1 September 1881): 2.

22. *Hennepin County Mirror* 11 (18 June 1881): 8.

23. *American Grange Bulletin and Scientific Farmer* 23 (23 September 1897): 2.

24. Hebb, "The Woman Movement in the California State Grange," 49–50, 80; *Journal of Proceedings of the Thirteenth Annual Session of the Pennsylvania State Grange*, 1885, 334–36; *Journal of Proceedings of the Twenty-First Annual Session of the Ohio State Grange 1983* (Sandusky: State Grange, 1893), 65; *Journal of Proceedings of the Fifteenth Annual Session Missouri State Grange 1887* (Sedalia: State Grange, 1887), 24–25.

25. Warren J. Gates, "Modernization As A Function Of An Agricultural Fair: The Great Grangers' Picnic Exhibition At Williams Grove, Pennsylvania, 1873–1916," *Agricultural History* 58 (July 1984): 262–79; Gates, "Her Voices At The Picnic: Women's Programs At Williams Grove, The 1890s," a paper presented at the Zatae Longsdorff Conference in Women's Studies, 1978.

26. *Farmer's Friend and Grange Advocate* 18 (4 July 1891): 4.

27. Ibid. 18 (10 October 1891): 2, 5.

28. Ibid. 19 (24 September 1892): 1, (1 October 1892): 1; (22 October 1892): 1. (29 October 1892): 1.

29. Ibid. 29 (2 January 1901): 1.

30. *American Grange Bulletin and Scientific Farmer* 23 (3 February 1898): 10.

31. *The Husbandman* 8 (11 January 1882): 2; (25 January 1882): 2; (1 February 1882): 2.

32. *Bulletin* 5 (October 1879).

33. *The Husbandman* 8 (20 August 1881): 2.

34. Flora Kimball, "The Bread Winners of Briarfield," with other Kimball clippings in the National City, California Public Library.

35. *Grange Visitor* 3 (15 November 1878): 7; 4 (15 January 1879): 7.

36. Ibid. 7 (5 April 1894): 3; Calvert, "The Southern Grange," 148–49.

37. *Pennsylvania Grange News* 2 (February 1906): 6–7.

38. Typescript report in Archives of the Maryland State Grange in the Historical Manuscripts and Archives Department, University of Maryland College Park Libraries.

39. Theodora Penny Martin, *The Sound of Our Own Voices: Women's Study Clubs 1860–1910* (Boston: Beacon Press, 1987), especially Chapter 5.

40. *Grange Visitor* 6 (15 June 1880): 7.

41. *National Grange* 4 (19 May 1909): 12.

42. *The Husbandman* 6 (31 March 1880): 2. Glenna Matthews, *"Just a Housewife": The Rise and Fall of Domesticity in America* (New York: Oxford University Press, 1987), 14–17, 65 persuasively argues that domestic craft traditions really were important sources of pride. According to Matthews, nineteenth-century literature that took those traditions seriously gave women "a sense of efficacy."

43. Ibid.; (14 January 1880): 2; *Grange Visitor* 17 (1 September 1892): 6; *American Grange Bulletin and Scientific Farmer* 24 (15 December 1898): 10.

44. *Indiana Farmer* 13 (9 February 1878): 6.

45. Ibid. 12 (17 February 1877): 7.

46. *The Husbandman* 6 (17 December 1879): 2; (31 December 1879): 2; (7 January 1880): 2.

47. Ibid. 3 (22 November 1876): 2.

48. *Grange Visitor* 11 (1 September 1886): 6.

49. *The Husbandman* 8 (15 February 1882): 2.

50. Ibid. 1 (13 January 1875): 3.

51. *American Grange Bulletin and Scientific Farmer* 24 (27 October 1898): 10–11.

52. Ibid.; *Bulletin* 3 (November 1876).

53. *American Grange Bulletin and Scientific Farmer* 32 (26 March 1903): 10.

54. *Grange Visitor* 10 (15 March 1884): 6.

55. Ibid. 6 (15 March 1887): 6.

56. *The Husbandman* 3 (13 December 1876): 2; *Bulletin* 2 (November 1876); *Grange Visitor* 6 (1 November 1880): 6.

57. *Farmer's Friend and Grange Advocate* 19 (25 June 1891): 1.

58. This will be discussed in the next chapter.

59. *Bulletin* 4 (November 1878).

60. *The Husbandman* 2 (15 September 1875): 2.

61. *Grange Visitor* 3 (3 June 1877): 6.

62. *American Grange Bulletin and Scientific Farmer* 33 (31 December 1903): 10.

63. *Bulletin* 2 (November 1876).

64. *National Grange* 2 (15 July 1908): 12.

65. Buell, *One Woman's Work for Farm Women*, 9.

66. *The Husbandman* 15 (12 June 1889): 2.

67. *Grange Visitor* 3 (May 1877): 5.

68. Grosh, *Mentor in the Granges and Homes of Patrons of Husbandry*, 124–25.

69. *Indiana Farmer* 12 (31 March 1877): 7.

70. *Pacific Rural Press* 21 (14 May 1881): 346.

71. *Grange Visitor* 6 (15 February 1880): 6.

72. "What the Grange Has Meant to Me," *The Country Gentleman* 82 (1 December 1917): 36–38.

73. It parallels the argument of "Does Woman Need the Grange?" an undated but earlier leaflet issued by the National Grange Lecture Department and held in the National Agricultural Library. Composed as a dialogue, the leaflet concerns a young woman who had attended a town high school and then returned to her parents' farm. She complained to her mother of "this unbroken round of housework, seldom seeing any but home faces except on Sundays." The point, as of the *Country Gentleman* piece, was that drudgery especially distressed young women whose educations had acquainted them with different possibilities, and that it drove them away from farming.

4

Drudgery and Home
Economics

One virtue of the Grange, a member suggested in 1873, was that "it elevates us poor trodden down females."[1] Earlier agricultural societies and farmers' clubs meant to educate and dignify farm men; the Grange continued that mission and also called for "a proper appreciation of the abilities and sphere of woman."[2] That sentiment was unoriginal, in fact resoundingly conventional, but Grangers said that the respect due to women needed special emphasis among farmers. Too many farm women were so "trodden down" by drudgery that they were unable to discharge the highest responsibilities that belonged to their "sphere." Such women, a critical but sympathetic sister told the Pennsylvania State Grange in 1885, planted no flowers, served cheerless meals in noisome kitchens, and "condemned all things beautiful, and those that had any love for a better life." She thought that progressive farm women, certainly many Grangers, had attained a higher level of domesticity, but that too many farm families continued to live brutishly because overworked women failed in their most important responsibilities.[3]

Grangers and other critics of rural life routinely insisted that mindless, repetitive, exhausting drudgery was farm women's most basic problem. Anson Bartlett made that point two years before he pressed Oliver Hudson Kelley to devise roles for women in the Grange. Describing the hard work that women had to do on Ohio dairy farms, Bartlett wondered if "any woman can be found who can endure as much" as the typical woman dairy farmer had to bear "even for a single season, to say nothing of a term of years, and retain the semblance of health and strength."[4] Similarly, the Reverend Aaron Grosh, first Chaplain of the National Grange, wrote a few years later that farm women spent their days at hard labor "in the heated, steaming kitchen" with only "children and domestics" for company. Even on Sundays, when men got some leisure and social enjoyment, women had to cook and attend "to the extra demands of the 'men-folks.' "[5]

Few Grangers saw any need to amend that description of farm women's plight at any time in their Order's first half-century. They continued to identify drudgery as the root of all evil in farm homes even as new appliances speeded household tasks and the "de-feminization" of agriculture reduced women's farm work.[6] They were probably right to do so. The new appliances were efficient, certainly, but encouraged women to raise their standards of housekeeping rather than reducing their labor; sewing and washing machines meant more elaborate sewing and frequent laundry than women had formerly done.[7] And U.S. Department of Agriculture studies demonstrate that the "de-feminization" of agriculture did not stop farm women from doing a great deal of hard work, both outdoors and in their houses, well into the twentieth century. For example, a 1920 survey showed that 89 percent of farm women in the central states looked after poultry, 68 percent fetched water from outdoor pumps, 54 percent carried wood and coal, 67 percent gardened, 45 percent milked cows, 66 percent made butter, and 22 percent did field work. Because the Farm Bureau and the Extension Service, which gathered the survey data, "usually reached the more prosperous and 'progressive' farm homes," that last figure is probably low.[8] Similarly, a 1929 U.S. Department of Agriculture study of tasks performed by women on various kinds of farms around the country reported that new appliances really had eased some chores but that women got less help than they previously had from other members of their families, so they worked just as hard as they had fifty years before. They put in sixty-three hours a week, on average. Eleven hours and thirteen minutes went to dairy, poultry, and garden work; food preparation took twenty-five hours and fifty-one minutes; housecleaning required eight hours and fifteen minutes; laundry and other chores took the remaining time. Since the standard industrial work week was then forty-two hours, the study concluded that farm women really were overworked.[9]

The 1929 survey was interesting enough to merit an extended summary in Pennsylvania's Grange journal but said nothing of substance that Grangers had not repeated, with little variation, since Anson Bartlett bemoaned the condition of women dairy farmers. Drudgery, Grangers routinely said, was the central problem of farm women's lives. It isolated too many of them from the society of their peers, kept them from developing their minds and creating gracious homes, and repelled young women, especially those whose educations had acquainted them with better possibilities.[10]

Of course, other people worked hard, too. But Grangers and other critics of rural life thought that farm women were more likely than either town women or their own men to get trapped in continual drudgery. Eliza Gifford, for example, told her fellow New York Grangers that rich men in cities sometimes worked hard, but maintained their wives in leisure, and that urban workmen's wives were free of the outdoor work that farm women had to do. Moreover, Gifford observed, town women had ready access to baker's bread and other prepared foods, while farm cooks had to bake, dry apples and corn, can fruit, render lard, and make sausage.[11] As for farm women's disadvantages relative to farm men, Grangers observed that men were more likely to hire hands to help with their own work than to assist in their wives' and found more opportunities to get away from their farms.[12] A Pennsylvania woman, speaking to her Grange in 1894, reminded men that they were "free to go to the store or to the neighbors and chat half a day and your work goes on just the same." The men she knew had hired hands and liberty; their wives labored alone from dawn until dusk and into the night.[13] Marie Howland once suggested that farmers' daughters were less stultified than their sons because they had a greater variety of tasks, but the preponderance of opinion held that women's work was more oppressive than men's.[14]

Sometimes Grange women applied that generalization to their own lives. In 1880, for example, a Wisconsin sister told readers of the state Grange *Bulletin* how depressed she was by her hard work and her husband's callousness. On a typical day, she prepared an elaborate breakfast, churned butter, baked bread and pie, picked string beans, fed chickens, made pot cheese, sewed part of a new shirt for her husband, picked currants, served dinner and supper, and finally made beds, which she had somehow forgotten to do in the morning. Her husband added to her burdens by producing an unexpected supper guest and then requiring that his coat be mended so that he could accompany his friend to town for the evening. At the end of it all, she wrote, "My head aches, my back aches, and my heart aches." She fully understood "why farmers' wives go crazy."[15]

Few Grange women expressed such desperate unhappiness. Many of the women who wrote and spoke in Grange forums led relatively fortunate lives and knew it. Others reported specific problems, but in a matter-of-fact tone, which suggested that they were bearing up well and took pride in their fortitude. "Lovica" told New York's Grange journal that she did a lot of hard farm work because her husband was a "little fellow" and lacked other help, but she showed no sign of breaking under the strain. Her letter remarked on a problem—that she had little time to write—but also implied very clearly and proudly that she was strong enough to bear her burdens.[16] Similarly, a Mississippi woman told her Grange that she had little time to write or study and that one of her children, trying to describe another woman, said that "she had a wilted face just like yours and Mrs. B's." The child's observation stung, but its mother responded with determination to write for the Grange, read, grow flowers, and lead the most cultivated life that she could under her circumstances. Wilting drudgery did not defeat her.[17]

Grangers admired such strength. One of Mary Mayo's contributions to the Michigan *Grange Visitor* describes a noble old woman whose hands were gnarled by work, whose "whole life had been a labor of love for others."[18] Excessive work could be harmful, Mayo said in many places, but she respected women who labored hard without complaint. Jennie Buell considered Mayo herself a model of serene fortitude. Many Grange women were just as exemplary. They sometimes described their own problems but rarely invited pity. Occasionally, they even suggested that women's tribulations were fit subjects of humor.

A Pennsylvania sister did that in a long speech to her county, or Pomona, Grange in 1891. She began by apologizing for her lack of preparation and literary polish, though neither deficiency is apparent in the published version of her speech. After all, she said, a "woman's time for leisure and mental cultivation is mostly after nine o'clock in the evening and before five in the morning." She also promised to leave political subjects to the men because they had "opportunities to cultivate their minds and discuss and investigate political affairs at the post office and blacksmith shop on rainy afternoons that we women do not enjoy." Then she asked the brothers to reflect on their responsibility for women's drudgery. "Remember when you courted your wife, and were so devoted that you wanted to die for her, and she wouldn't let you, but after she had married you and found out what sort of man you were she was willing you should, and then you backed out and wouldn't do it?" Since then, "you have not tried to lighten her burdens" but have reduced her to a " 'hewer of wood and a drawer of water.' " Finally, she assured them that they could do better. "Passable husbands," she observed, "are sometimes made out of extremely poor material."[19]

That speech began by identifying its author as a victim of drudgery and isolation; it said that her hard life had kept her from writing a better speech, though her wit and graceful writing obviously softened that point. The accusation that men had not tried to lighten their wives' burdens darkened her tone briefly, but then she concluded humorously. Her speech was a good-natured performance, made some serious points, and suggested that she had her personal sufferings well under control.

At least one male Granger, quite possibly just one, addressed women's problems in the same tone. In 1914, the pseudonymous John Plowshare described a fictitious, or at least broadly caricatured, local Grange debate on equal suffrage that his wife interrupted by saying that she "had more interest in having things conveniently arranged about the farm" than in the question on the floor. She then asked the assembled brothers and sisters what they thought of a husband who compelled her "to do the washing on an old fashioned wash-board, wring the clothes out by hand, pump and carry the water, lug the swill into the field, chop the wood with a dull axe, churn the butter with a paddle, and finally, mow the lawn with a sheepshears." Plowshare, badly embarrassed, could only defend himself by saying that he was no worse than other men in the community. His report of his wife's speech catalogued some real problems, while suggesting that Grangers could deal with such matters humorously.[20] And his wife's complaints were a fair approximation of what Grange women really did say about men, sometimes about their husbands in particular. A Michigan woman complained that they were too slow to plow kitchen gardens in the spring; a New Yorker said that they showed too little appreciation of their wives; and a Wisconsin sister held that it was tyrannical of men to control the entirety of farm income and spend it all on their own pleasures and interests.[21]

Complaints about men's exclusive control of money were particularly common. It contributed to drudgery by making expenditures for household conveniences less likely than purchases of farm implements. It also implied that women's hard work was less valuable than men's. Farms should be partnerships, many women argued, and husbands and wives should share financial responsibility. But too many men behaved as if they alone were responsible for their farms' earnings. An Indiana sister put that in the gentlest way imaginable in a speech to her Grange. She asked the members to envision the ideal farmer of the coming twentieth century. He would treat his wife as a partner, "and she will feel entitled to an equal share of all that their united energies may earn." In that good future, no farm woman would have to sell butter and eggs behind her husband's back to get a little money. The speaker implied, very clearly, that the Hoosier present fell considerably short of that high standard of mutuality.[22] Similarly, though far less gently, a Wisconsin woman told readers of the state's Grange *Bulletin* that women had recently helped to decide how her local Grange was to pay the rent on its hall. She thought it was "simply ludicrous for the sisters to vote to pay rent when there is not one woman in a hundred that has anything to pay rent with." The women she knew had to go to their husbands for money. They hated that, and so did the writer, who apparently shared the general indignity.[23]

Most of the Grange women who complained about men's exclusive control of money said nothing explicit about how it was handled on their own farms. They might have been describing their own problems, or they might have been criticizing the practices of less enlightened families. At least one woman made absolutely clear that she was doing the latter. She managed part of her farm, she told a meeting of her northern Indiana Grange, and took the proceeds as her own; "it gives me a more independent feeling," she remarked with obvious satisfaction. The rest of her speech urged other families to adopt the same arrangement, making sure that women got half of the farm income. Her purpose, clearly, was not to air a personal grievance. She was proud, not aggrieved, and the overt burden of her speech was advice to less fortunate women.[24]

Grangers claimed to know about farm women who were distinctly less fortunate than themselves, whose hard lives had driven them mad. Critics of rural life had been warning about farm women's risk of madness at least since 1862 when W. W. Hall, a well-known health pundit, contributed an essay about the menace to the U.S. Commissioner of Agriculture's annual report. Hall claimed that an unspecified "agricultural state" then had 607 patients in its insane asylum, of whom thirty-nine were farmers' wives and sixteen were farmers' daughters; "no other class of wives or daughters is half as numerous!" Then he drew a conclusion that is not clearly supported by his numbers—that farm women were overrepresented among the insane. A romantic myth portrayed rural womanhood as an idyll of "beauty and innocence and exuberant health," but too often, Hall wrote, reality was a "pale and wan and haggard face, half covered by long black hair, and coal black eyes peering hotly on you from behind the bars and grates of a dark prison-house."[25]

The idea that farm women were especially liable to mental illness proved durable. A prominent Populist woman thought that farm women were more likely to lose their minds than were members of any other occupational group and that isolation and drudgery were to blame; a Wisconsin Grange woman guessed in 1878 that half of the inmates in insane asylums were farmers' wives; another Wisconsin sister, writing two years later, said that she fully understood "why farmers' wives go crazy"; a Pennsylvania woman told her county Grange in 1901 that she had "read one day where there are more farmers' wives who go insane than any other class of people"; and Elizabeth Patterson, founder of the National Grange home economics committee, reported in 1910 that "there are more women from the farm in insane asylums than from any other walk of life."[26] Similar statements appeared in letters from farm women sent to the United States Department of Agriculture after Secretary Houston asked for information about their conditions in 1913. The person who edited the final report, which consisted mainly of excerpts from their letters, noted that a Department statistician had investigated such statements for twenty years and had never been able to substantiate them. In fact, the numbers seemed to "indicate that the percentage of insane women who come from farms is below rather than above the average."[27]

Statistics to the contrary notwithstanding, Grangers discerned reasons why farming produced more than its share of mentally ill women. Its "endless chain of routine" has long crushed "the life and spirit of our sisters," a Michigan Grange woman wrote, and a New York sister argued that "the very nature of farm life entails certain conditions that are inevitable, and their tendency is to shut in and enfetter a woman's life until soul-life . . . becomes narrow, distorted, and unfruitful." The New Yorker thought that the Grange could reduce the damage but that drudgery and isolation would certainly exact their price. She entirely agreed with Marx and Engels about the inherent "idiocy of rural life," though she did not borrow their striking phrase.[28]

Few Grangers went anywhere nearly that far. Typically, they said that farming was potentially healthy and even ennobling. Direct criticisms of farming aroused loyal defenders, such as the woman who told her New York county Grange that she had heard a town woman say that farmers' intellectual horizons were limited to the care of animals; she answered that with real outrage. A week after the New York Grange journal printed her talk, it carried an essay in which another woman told another county Grange that "agriculture is the most ancient as well as the most useful occupation of man."[29] Grangers knew the formulae. Farming was not idiotic; it was, at least potentially, a noble calling that deserved far more respect than it got. Grangers regularly demanded that respect and tried to earn it by showing how cultivated farmers could be.

No inherent flaws in rural life created women's predicament, Grangers said. Its causes, easily identified and corrected, were farm people themselves. If they changed, as Grangers often claimed to have done, or to have begun doing, rural life could reach its beautiful potential. Farm men especially needed to change because all too many of the less progressive among them were inconsiderate of their wives and daughters. W. W. Hall stated that accusation in detail. He thought that farmers oppressed their wives by expecting them to carry water long distances from pump to kitchen, sleeping at night while tired women got up to care for sick children, not keeping houses in repair, speaking to their wives disrespectfully in front of children and hands, and never saying a word of encouragement or appreciation. Hall was particularly troubled about laundry. Women should not have done that hot, heavy job without help, but they usually did.[30]

Grangers identified some of the same abuses, but their criticisms of farm men were generally less harsh than Hall's. Maine's Grange organ reprinted another journal's opinion that farmers showed less appreciation of women than did men of other classes because of their ignorance; other Grangers observed that some unprogressive men still made their daughters do field work, which took the girls "out of their proper sphere," and forgot that work is healthy only in moderation and that it "is not just or good or noble to wear out the wife of your bosom."[31] But Grangers generally treated farm men with a degree of sympathy, at least more than Hall showed, and often suggested that women bore a share of the blame for their own plight. Grange women, especially, argued that farm wives often worked harder than was really necessary.

The household hints published in the women's departments of Grange journals clearly implied what some of the sisters said directly—that farm women were inefficient or did unnecessary work. Reducing drudgery, Mary Mayo suggested, could be as easy as serving fresh apples instead of pie. A more radical idea, which appeared first in Maine's Grange journal and then in Wisconsin's, was that women who had more cream than they could make into butter without overwork should feed the surplus to their pigs. Losing cream might distress their husbands at first, but the writer blithely predicted that the men would soon learn to keep fewer cows.[32] Such helpful hints implied that women controlled their own work. Brutish men might value pies and butter more than their wives' well-being, but women were sovereign within their own sphere. If they wore themselves out with baking and churning, they should accept at least part of the blame. A Skaneatles, New York, woman put that forcefully in a speech to the Onondaga County Pomona Grange in 1888. She called rural women's compulsive attention to household details their "besetting sin" and urged them to take time for "mental improvement" so that they could command their children's respect.[33] The women she had in mind could work less and read more if they chose; they were willfully, sinfully, busy and ignorant.

Some early twentieth-century Grange women, enthusiasts of scientific domesticity, observed a kind of obscurantism in farm homes. Dr. Hannah McK. Lyons, a physician who chaired the Pennsylvania State Grange home economics committee, illustrated that failing with a story told by Martha Van Rensselaer, a home economics lecturer at Cornell. After one of Van Rensselaer's public talks, a farm couple came up to the front of the room because the man wanted to know how to get one of the self-heating irons that the lecture had commended. He hoped that it would save his wife from having to do her ironing over a hot stove. But his wife impatiently said, " 'Never mind, Thomas, we don't want one o' them at our house.' "[34] Writing to the same point, another Pennsylvania woman described a farm wife who refused to leave her home for seven years and then spent a few hours away just to give "herself the gruesome pleasure of attending a neighbor's funeral." The woman who told that story blamed much of the insanity among farm women on such irrational behavior. She assumed that women had enough control over their work to arrange their lives in healthy, reasonable ways.[35]

They could decide to do less work, which would require them to make a reasoned distinction "between essentials and non-essentials." Elizabeth Patterson, first chairman of the National Grange home economics committee, thought that women subjected themselves to unnecessary work because they had not learned to make that distinction. She especially decried the "superfluity of pies, cakes, and preserves" in farm homes; women who took the trouble to understand their families' real nutritional needs would spend less effort packing them with calories and more on their esthetic and moral nurture.[36] Focusing on essential work was the first step in defeating drudgery. Then, Patterson and many others said, women should learn to do their necessary work efficiently, which meant analyzing tasks and applying new methods instead of plodding along in their mothers' footsteps.

Encouraging such intelligent domesticity was one object of the many household hints that Grange women offered to each other and it was the great purpose of domestic science or home economics, the discipline that they expected to free women from mindless drudgery, just as agricultural science was supposed to lift farmers out of traditional ruts. Particularly impressed by the mix of applied science and general education that had become available in the new agricultural colleges, Grangers urged that women be given, and fully exploit, a parallel kind of instruction. Domestic science led by the agricultural colleges was an official Grange objective from the 1870s onward and something approaching a crusade, under the name home economics, early in this century. Enthusiasts such as Patterson and Lyons considered it the great panacea for both drudgery and young farm women's educational neglect.

The Order at least formally supported domestic science by 1874 when its Declaration of Purposes, which called for a "proper appreciation of the abilities and sphere of woman" and enhancement of the "comforts and attractions of our homes," asked the agricultural colleges to teach "practical agriculture, domestic science, and all of the arts which adorn the home." Practical agriculture came first in that series as it did in the esteem of most Grange leaders. In 1886, for example, Master J. H. Hale of the Connecticut State Grange showed what his priorities were by protesting Yale's control of the state's land grant fund on the ground that few "farmers' boys" met Yale's admission requirements. He wanted the fund transferred to the agricultural school at Storrs, now the University of Connecticut, which did not "exclude any good, bright farm boy of proper age."[37] The sister who led the woman's work committee of the New Hampshire Grange saw the same low level of concern about practical education for women in her state. In a uniquely harsh 1890 report, she accused the state Grange of denying women opportunities for real leadership in the organization, and then called that a "trivial" failing "compared with the fact that we are not working for our daughters' welfare as we are for our sons.' " The New Hampshire State Grange was pressing for a real agricultural college independent of Dartmouth but did not protest New Hampshire's lack of a school where young women could learn "the chemistry of cooking, or the art of house-keeping, the making of marketable cheese, or gilt-edged butter, home sanitation, and mechanical arts." Admitting women to an agricultural college would not be enough; she demanded that they be offered courses appropriate to their vocation.[38]

Grange advocates of vocational, domestic instruction for women modeled their argument on the already familiar case for agricultural education. The basic premise of both was that young people should study their future work rather than doing without much education or having to settle for education that would do them no practical good. Thomas Green Fessenden, editor of the *New England Farmer*, made that point repeatedly throughout the first third of the nineteenth century. He ridiculed New England's proliferating academies for teaching farm boys a few useless scraps of Latin along with the idea that scholars of their erudition were too good for productive work.[39] Ezra Carr, an early California Grange leader, professor of agriculture and horticulture at the University of California, and husband of Jeanne Carr, applied the same argument to women. His 1875 book on the Grange included an extended discussion of "The Industrial Education of Women," which claimed that they had been denied useful instruction even though the importance of their work had been universally recognized since Proverbs celebrated the virtuous housewife whose price was far above rubies. Carr regarded the "average female seminary" just as Fessenden viewed academies, and he quoted another critic who wrote that their chief purpose was to furnish " 'intelligent playthings for men possessing exhaustless wealth.' " Carr insisted that women were not toys but had their own valuable work in which they should be trained.

Jeanne Carr, who offered resolutions favoring various kinds of practical education to the California State Grange meeting of 1874, fully shared her husband's educational ideas.[40] In the same spirit, Mary Mayo strongly supported both agricultural education and domestic science. She told an 1880 farmers' institute that the right kind of education was precious but that useless learning, by which she meant ancient languages and mathematics, produced a taste for useless things, which she called extravagance. Unlike a Wisconsin contemporary, who thought that mathematics and the classics would not impair women's cooking and churning, Mayo considered such attainments pernicious. All education should be practical; it should enhance people's moral characters and vocational skills. So she waged a long campaign for domestic science at her state's agriculture college. Parents, she said, were as "anxious that

their daughters shall be . . . trained for the practical work of their lives"
as they were to have their sons trained in agriculture.[41]

Carr, Mayo, and other Grangers agreed with the fathers of agricultural
education that young people should prepare for their destined callings.
Rather than opening students' minds to a variety of possibilities, as
contemporary women's colleges meant to do, the advocates of practical
training said that schools should take their students' vocational destinies
for granted. Philip Emmanuel Von Fellenberg, a pioneer agricultural
educator in early nineteenth-century Switzerland, had made that explicit
by providing liberal education for upper-class students and farm training
for others. American advocates of agricultural education admired, imi-
tated, and criticized Von Fellenberg's program. They understood that it
would have to be modified in democratic America, but they never entirely escaped its social assumptions.[42] And supporters of the parallel
kind of women's education did not either. An 1879 essay in the Wisconsin State Grange *Bulletin* demonstrated the continuing force of Von
Fellenberg's ideas by criticizing the common American faith in education
as a vehicle for upward mobility. In fact, it argued, most people could
never "rise out of ordinary, useful labor into high position." Too many
women, it continued, were "striving for genteel employments, who
would be a thousand times better in body and mind, if they were engaged in housework."[43]

The agricultural colleges that Grangers admired so much, in which
many of them wanted to make room for women, mostly began within
a few years of the Civil War. Michigan Agricultural College, now Michigan State University, opened in 1857; Farmers' High School, now Pennsylvania State University, opened in 1859; other such institutions began
after Congress passed the famous Morrill Act in 1862. Rather than found-
ing new colleges, some of the states at first gave their land grant funds
to existing institutions that agreed to create departments of agriculture.
Agricultural education, in various forms, with greater and lesser degrees
of public support, spread across the country within a generation, but
rarely did it make much provision for women.

The Iowa State College, now Iowa State University, was an early
exception. It offered "Domestic Economy" as part of its "Ladies'
Course," starting in 1871. A few years later, the State Agricultural College of Kansas, now Kansas State University, offered "courses in 'Household Management and Economy,' 'The Management of Children and
Their Private Instruction,' and 'A Knowledge of the Laws of Health and
Nursing the Sick.' " More such courses appeared in various agricultural
colleges through the remaining years of the nineteenth century, but only
2,000 of the 61,000 women enrolled in various coeducational institutions
of higher education in 1900 were concentrating on domestic subjects,

while 43,000 were studying pedagogy. Home economics became a really popular and widely available curriculum only in the early twentieth century, when its spread in lower schools created a demand for home economics teachers.[44] Before that happened, Grangers, particularly Grange women, criticized the agricultural colleges for neglecting the practical study of domestic work.

The Michigan Agricultural College got a full measure of that criticism. Its charter required offerings in domestic science, but when the state Grange sent a committee of five women and four men to visit the college in 1877, it had no such courses and few women students. The Grange committee noted that women were attending the university at Ann Arbor and the state normal schools but that the college was virtually closed to them. The few college women pursued the usual agricultural course; the faculty distinguished them from male students only by assigning them practical work in horticulture instead of agriculture—which meant that they set tomato plants, picked potato bugs, and did other such chores—and admiring their looks. The college severely limited their numbers starting in 1872, when it rejected sixteen of its twenty women applicants, taking only the four who could live at home, because men needed all of the college housing. The state Board of Agriculture, which governed the college, claimed to want women students but said that they could be accommodated in large numbers only after a dormitory had been built for them. The Grange committee responded by urging the legislature to fund a dormitory; Michigan Grangers reiterated that demand until it was met in 1899. Then Michigan lawmakers rewarded intense lobbying by women's clubs and the Grange with a $95,000 appropriation, which was one-third of the value of existing college property and 10 percent more than the college had requested. The college began a "Women's Course of Study" three years earlier. It included domestic skills, calisthenics, and music, along with "modern languages, literature and such other studies" as were thought to develop "broad-minded, cultured women." Mary Mayo, according to the historian of home economics at Michigan State, was the "influential energetic leader" of the agitation for that course. The college honored her several contributions in 1931, when it dedicated Mary Mayo Hall, a dormitory for women.[45]

Grangers were particularly effective at Michigan State but made broadly similar efforts on behalf of women's education at other colleges. In 1902, for example, the Delaware State Grange passed a resolution favoring coeducation at Delaware College, now the University of Delaware, and ten years later supported a proposal by President George Harter to create a separate but affiliated women's college. During its 1912 meeting at Newark, just before the legislature acted on the proposal, the Delaware Grange heard a "parade of speakers" who supported the new institution. Then it joined the State Federation of Women's Clubs, the WCTU, and the Women's Equal Suffrage Association in cheering the proposal through the legislature. Dean Winifred Robinson, a botanist who had received her Ph.D. from Columbia University and taught at Vassar, quickly organized an institution that combined vocational training with science, athletics, English, and French. One of her first four professorial appointments went to home economics.[46]

Michigan State and Delaware participated in a rapid expansion of home economics instruction. The ten college home economics departments of 1895 became thirty by 1900 and forty-one by 1922.[47] The Grange contributed less to the expansion than did the rising demand for home economics teachers in public schools, but its women applauded the discipline's growth and worked to diffuse its lessons. Lecturers studied home economics bulletins from the agricultural colleges and led discussions about their topics; Grange leaders, such as Elizabeth Patterson and Hannah McK. Lyons, saw that an abundance of information and advice from college home economics departments got into Grange publications.

Home economics was a crusade for those women because it promised to solve the old problems of drudgery and isolation. Grangers had long said that women were exhausted, stultified, and even maddened by their excessive work. Drudgery blighted farm homes, they said, because it prevented women from attaining their highest domestic possibilities. So they tried to help overworked women by exhorting them to distinguish between necessary and unnecessary tasks, and to do the former efficiently. Home economics preached the same gospel but with the awesome authority of science.[48] That authority, Grange women trusted, made it the sovereign cure for drudgery.

NOTES

1. Sarah Margaret Stephenson, "The Social and Educational Aspects of the Grange, 1870–1934" (M.A. thesis, University of Wisconsin, 1935), 19.

2. Gardner, *The Grange*, 519.

3. *Journal of Proceedings of the Thirteenth Annual Session of the Pennsylvania State Grange*, 1885, 34–36.

4. Jones, *History of Agriculture in Ohio to 1880*, 188.

5. Grosh, *Mentor in the Granges and Homes of Patrons of Husbandry*, 122.

6. Bengt Ankarloo, "Agriculture and Women's Work: Directions of Change in the West, 1700–1900," *Journal of Family History* 5 (Summer 1979): 111–20 is a very broad description of "de-feminization." Sally McMurry, *Families and Farmhouses in 19th Century America* (New York: Oxford University Press, 1988), especially Chapter 4, applies that idea to progressive American farm families.

7. Ruth Schwartz Cowan, *More Work for Mother: The Ironies of Household Technology from the Open Hearth to the Microwave* (New York: Basic Books, 1983), 98–99; McMurry, *Families and Farmhouses*, 96; Matthews, *"Just A Housewife"*, 111 generalizes that "time spent in housework declined little if at all in the first two-

thirds of the twentieth century"; Fink, *Open Country Iowa*, 47 points out that farm women got much less help from new appliances in the early twentieth century than did their urban counterparts. In 1920, only 21% of Iowa farm homes had electricity. The proportion increased to 45% in 1940, when 75% of the homes in the particular part of Iowa that Fink describes still lacked running water.

8. Neth, "Preserving the Family Farm," 36-768.

9. *Pennsylvania Grange News* 26 (November 1929): 8.

10. See, for example, "Does Woman Need the Grange?" an undated leaflet issued by the National Grange Lecture Department, in the National Agricultural Library.

11. Untitled, undated speech in Eliza Gifford's manuscripts, Patterson Library and Art Gallery.

12. *Dirigo Rural* 3 (24 June 1876): 4.

13. *Farmer's Friend and Grange Advocate* 21 (29 September 1894): 1.

14. Howland, "The Patrons of Husbandry," 340.

15. *Bulletin* 6 (2 August 1880): 3.

16. *The Husbandman* 8 (20 August 1881): 2.

17. *American Grange Bulletin and Scientific Farmer* 21 (3 September 1896): 10–11.

18. *Grange Visitor* 11 (16 November 1885): 6.

19. *Farmer's Friend and Grange Advocate* 18 (3 October 1891): 6; Neth, "Preserving the Family Farm," 364, 376 suggests that such criticisms of men's failure to be helpful were just. Though farm men sometimes shared women's chores by hauling water for laundry, or helping to churn, work sharing "usually meant women doing men's work rather than vice versa."

20. *Pennsylvania Grange News* 9 (July 1914).

21. *Grange Visitor* 8 (15 August 1882): 6; *The Husbandman* 15 (5 December 1888): 2; *Bulletin* 4 (December 1878).

22. *American Grange Bulletin and Scientific Farmer* 21 (28 May 1896): 10.

23. *Bulletin* 4 (December 1878).

24. *American Grange Bulletin and Scientific Farmer* 21 (28 May 1896): 2.

25. Hall, "Hardships of Farmers' Wives," 462.

26. Wagner, "Farms, Families, and Reform," 147–48; *Bulletin* 4 (August 1878); Ibid. 6 (2 August 1880): 3; *Farmer's Friend and Grange Advocate* 28 (21 December 1901): 4; *National Grange Monthly* 8 (January 1911): 10.

27. *Social and Labor Needs of Farm Women*, 24.

28. *Grange Visitor* 3 (1 February 1878): 6; *Farmer's Friend and Grange Advocate* 25 (23 April 1898): 6; Karl Marx and Friedrich Engels, "Manifesto of the Communist Party" in Lewis S. Feuer, ed., *Marx and Engels, Basic Writings on Politics and Philosophy* (New York: Anchor Books, 1959), 11.

29. *The Husbandman* 15 (12 June 1889): 2; (19 June 1889): 4.

30. Hall, "Hardships of Farmers' Wives," 462–64.

31. *Farmer's Friend and Grange Advocate* 19 (25 June 1892): 1; Dudley W. Adams, *Address to the Patrons of Muscatine and Union Counties*, Bryan Fund Publication No. 8 (N.p.: National Grange, 1872[?]); David B. Danbom, *The Resisted Revolution: Urban America and the Industrialization of Agriculture, 1900–1930* (Ames: The Iowa State University Press, 1979), 84–85, similarly notes that early twentieth century farm women occasionally joined in the Country Life Movement's criticisms of

farmers for imposing drudgery on their wives, but more typically "jumped to their husbands' defense, noting that improvements were difficult and expensive and that farmers usually did their best to provide their families with comfort and convenience."

32. See discussion of Grange women's pronouncements on housekeeping and cooking in Chapter 3 and *Bulletin* 5 (January 1879).

33. *Husbandman* 15 (19 September 1888): 2.

34. *Pennsylvania Grange News* 9 (August 1912): 57.

35. Ibid. 4 (August 1907): 41–42.

36. *National Grange Monthly* 8 (January 1911): 10; Matthews, *"Just a Housewife"*, 112 criticizes home economists for failing to distinguish between really mindless drudgery and cherished crafts. Patterson's assault on elaborate cooking, which was fairly typical of Grange women from Mary Mayo onward, may exemplify Matthews' point.

37. Walter Stemmons, *Connecticut Agricultural College—A History* (Storrs: Connecticut Agricultural College, 1931), 65.

38. *Journal of Proceedings of the Seventeenth Annual Session of the New Hampshire State Grange*, 1890, 81–82.

39. Thomas Green Fessenden, *Original Poems* (Philadelphia: Lorenzo Press of E. Bronson, 1806), 140–41; *New England Farmer* 5 (9 August 1825): 27.

40. Ezra Carr, *The Patrons of Husbandry on the Pacific Coast* (San Francisco: A. L. Bancroft and Company, 1875), 385–86; Hebb, "The Woman Movement in the California State Grange," 92; Linda Fritschner, "The Rise and Fall of Home Economics" (Ph.D. diss., University of California at Davis, 1973), 61 quotes the language about "intelligent playthings" from a description of the "Women's Course" in the 1874 Kansas State Agricultural College Handbook.

41. *Nineteenth Annual Report of the Secretary of the State Board of Agriculture of the State of Michigan, 1880* (Kalamazoo: State Grange, 1880), 194–96; *Twelfth Annual Session of the Michigan State Grange*, 1885, 27.

42. Donald B. Marti, "The Purposes of Agricultural Education: Ideas and Projects in New York State, 1891–1965," *Agricultural History* 45 (October 1971): 274–75.

43. *Bulletin* 5 (June 1879).

44. Isabel Bevier, *Home Economics in Education* (Philadelphia: J. B. Lippincott Company, 1924), 122–27; Mabel Newcomer, *A Century of Higher Education for American Women* (New York: Harper and Brothers Publishers, 1959), 90.

45. *Grange Visitor* 2 (February 1877): 2–3; Madison Kuhn, *Michigan State: The First Hundred Years* (East Lansing: Michigan State University Press, 1955), 122–23, 211; Maude Gilchrist, *The First Three Decades of Home Economics at Michigan State College 1896–1926* (East Lansing: Michigan State College, 1947), 4, 8–9; Mary Mayo Hall dedication program and descriptive brochure in Michigan State University Archives and Historical Collection.

46. Joanne Passmore, *History of the Delaware State Grange* (N.p.: Delaware State Grange, 1975), 73, 76; John A. Munroe, *The University of Delaware: A History* (Newark: University of Delaware, 1986), 197, 201–2, 204–5.

47. Bevier, *Home Economics in Education*, 128.

48. The enthusiasm with which Grange women such as Lyons and Patterson promoted home economics was unalloyed. But the discipline's present repu-

tation among historians is problematical. Barbara Miller Solomon, *In the Company of Educated Women: A History of Women and Higher Education in America* (New Haven: Yale University Press, 1985), 85–87 briefly observes that women educators were deeply ambivalent about home economics in the period considered here. They saw it as a threat to real educational equality, but it employed "60 percent of women professors in coeducational schools" in 1911. Matthews, *"Just a Housewife"*, 161, sharply criticizes the whole movement but concedes that it "was genuinely helpful to farm women." Neth, "Preserving the Family Farm," 508, sees home economics as part of the "agricultural establishment's" promotion of urban-style separate spheres, an aspect of twentieth-century capitalism's assault on traditional rural communities. But Neth also suggests that the women who promoted home economics asserted "farm women's right to control and define their own labor, lessening patriarchal control of the family." Home economics' reputation is clouded, but scholars recognize that its promoters meant to help farm women and may actually have conferred some benefits on them.

5

Women's Committees

The Grange has always brought men and women together, but it has also expected them to fill different offices and talk about different subjects. Neither kind of specialization has ever been absolute; rural "mutuality" has always allowed some crossing of the line that separates men's and women's spheres. Grangers were particularly apt to cross that line starting in the 1890s, when women increased their share of the Order's working offices. But another kind of gender specialization became more rigid, or was at least more formally defined, a few years earlier when the Order began to create women's committees. The successors to those committees still direct women's Grange activities into channels that are considered appropriate to their gender. The committees' rhetoric and the projects that they have urged upon women indicate what those channels have been understood to be.

Efforts to define women's Grange work as distinct from Grange activities in general, and to give it a specific institutional locus, began sporadically in the 1870s. For example, the all-male resolutions committee of the 1874 Indiana State Grange observed that the "lady members" had not yet "taken the prominence really due them in the practical workings of the Order" and, therefore, proposed that all of the women in the state Grange be a committee to define women's tasks. The men wanted them to write a paper that could be sent to subordinate Granges around the state as a "guide for action."[1] Their proposal had no recorded consequences, and neither did Aaron Grosh's 1876 suggestion that all Granges with libraries appoint "one or two of the women, and the Lecturer and Librarian as a committee to see that no book of evil or even doubtful tendency" was allowed to reach their shelves.[2] As he demonstrated in other ways, too, Grosh considered women especially apt guardians of purity. Grangers also tried to define women's responsibilities, very tentatively, by appointing them to some of the Order's standing committees and omitting them from others. In 1880, for example, no women served on the National Grange committees responsible for cooperatives, transportation, and agriculture, but two served on the five-member committee on dormant Granges and three on the nine-member committee on the good of the Order.[3] Grangers also put women on committees responsible for education, social activities, and charitable work. In one Indiana Grange, which generally reserved active roles for men, women had half the places on the relief committee in 1888.[4] And the Iowa State Grange historian observed that women's committee participation increased in the 1880s, when the organization shifted its emphasis from cooperative enterprises and economic reforms to various social and educational endeavors.[5] Separation of women's responsibilities from men's weakened to a degree by the late 1880s, when state Granges generally included women on all committees, but Grangers continued to assume that women had special interests. At the end of the nineteenth century, when women served on all eighteen National Grange committees, they had ten out of twelve places on the education committee and dominated no other.[6]

Women were supposed to have distinctive interests, but nobody suggested that certain committees should consist of women exclusively until the Massachusetts State Grange created two women's committees in 1885. One, on household economy, reported that its subject was important enough to merit substantial shares of local Grange programs and urged Grange women to become "conspicuously efficient" housekeepers. The other, on "home entertainments and amusements," recommended that children be taught to appreciate good music and literature. Its general goal was to make "home so attractive that the children will have no longing after city life and pleasures."[7] All of that should have been perfectly familiar to anyone who had heard women speak at Grange meetings or read their contributions to Grange journals. The Massachusetts women innovated only by presenting those commonplace ideas as committee reports. The Connecticut State Grange committee on household economy, which began one year after the Massachusetts committees, produced the same kinds of exhortations.[8]

In 1887, the Massachusetts State Grange consolidated its two women's committees into a committee on "woman's special work in the Grange." Its report said that the Order's "wonderful prosperity" was largely due to women's efforts and then urged women to enhance the literary work and moral atmosphere of their Granges.[9] The Massachusetts example inspired the woman's work in the Grange committee that Addie S. Hale of South Glastonbury, Connecticut, persuaded the National Grange to begin in 1888. Hale became its first chairman, as the title always was, and immediately issued a circular that explained her intentions to the whole Order and called upon all state and local Granges to form like committees. Complaining that the Grange had made "little or no progress during the past year," it urged women to get the Order moving again. It recognized that women members had always worked hard but urged them to redouble their efforts through state and local woman's work committees. Their proper work was to "keep house in the Grange," which included calling on absentees, encouraging them to return, and helping the "lady officers" in their special duties. Almost as an afterthought, the circular suggested that the sisters might help other officers, too.[10]

The circular made some large, though innocuous, claims for Grange women. Their efforts, as the Massachusetts committee on woman's special work had also asserted, were absolutely vital to the Order. Women were responsible for its growth; they restored absent members to the fold, and they kept house, all of which meant that their Grange work was a straightforward extension of their domestic duties. In 1889, the committee extended its conception of domesticity, in a wholly conventional direction, by urging sisters to inform themselves "upon all legislative questions vital to the purity and intelligence of our homes," pursue legal equality of the sexes, and cooperate with other high-minded groups, especially the WCTU, in working for social purity. It also looked to the "time when our girls, as well as our boys, are admitted into all of our agricultural colleges."[11]

The national committee voiced general ideas, but it left their implementation to state committees, which in turn looked to their local counterparts. Just as the Master of the National Grange appointed members of the national committee, so state and local Masters filled their committees. Women did not necessarily ask to serve; sometimes they were conscripts, and they responded variously. Some, like Mary Mayo and the women who served with her on the woman's work committee of the Michigan State Grange, enthusiastically embraced the committee as a new kind of recognition for women that extended their opportunities to participate in the Grange; others, like the women who served on Rhode Island's belatedly organized committee, were obviously uncertain about what was expected of them. The Rhode Islanders' first report, in 1893, said that they were "working side by side with the brothers, encouraging with our presence and doing our part cheerfully." They hoped to submit more substantial reports later, which they finally did early in this century, after woman's work committees had disappeared from most other states.[12] Other women, particularly in Colorado, flatly opposed having a separate women's committee. A Colorado sister told the National Grange that it would make as much sense to have a men's

committee and actually proposed that one be formed. Rhode Island's
Master later told his organization that National Grange men "did not
take kindly" to the idea.[13]

Most states found a few women who were genuinely interested in
running their own special committees, but the enthusiasts were often
frustrated by other women's indifference or inaction. In Iowa, for example, three sisters divided the state into districts, as the national chairman recommended. The state chairman, who took the twenty-one
Granges in southwestern Iowa, reported after one year that several committees had raised money for local Grange activities. The most successful
earned $9.80 from a "Shadow Social" and other efforts. But most of the
Granges for which she was responsible produced no committee reports,
and the women responsible for the other two districts had also failed to
report, although she reminded them of their responsibility. She concluded that if the committee was to do "the good it might in our State,
some one will have to do more hard work in the future than has been
done in the past."[14]

In 1890, the Iowa committee again divided the state into districts and
gave local committees some more-or-less specific directions. They were
to call on absent members, recruit new members, help the women officers, involve children in Grange work, encourage temperance, and try
to improve the literary work of their local Granges. Again, few local
committees reported. One had conducted a recruiting drive, which it
considered successful, another had arranged Grange programs, and a
third had provided fruits and flowers for meetings. Finally, in 1894, the
state committee's long-suffering chairman recommended that her committee be discontinued. She had concluded that women did not understand what the committee asked them to do that was different from
what they had done before.[15] The chairman of Indiana's equally unsuccessful woman's work committee made the same point a little differently
when she said that a full description of woman's work "would be a
history of the Granges of Indiana."[16] Skeptical sisters thought that woman's work, unlike transportation or dormant Granges, was an insuffi-
ciently precise category to define a committee's charge.

Ohio's committee faced the same difficulty but found a specialty that
had lasting importance for Ohio Granges. In 1890, the committee reported that it had distributed roughly 450 national committee circulars
that invited reports of local activities but had heard from "a compara-
tively few" local committees. Seeking more information, the committee
held a meeting of women members of the state Grange, who reported
that sisters in one subordinate Grange had won all of its offices and that
twelve subordinates had observed children's days, which were supposed to interest children in the Order. Especially pleased with the
second report, the Ohio committee urged women to do everything pos-

sible to make Grange meetings interesting to children, and especially to organize juvenile Granges in association with their subordinates. Juvenile Granges, begun by Texas Grangers in 1888, had been given their own ritual by the 1890 National Grange. They became a favorite project of Grange women throughout the country, especially in Ohio.[17]

Michigan probably had the most energetic woman's work committee, though it began slowly. The state Grange created the committee, at Mary Mayo's initiative, early in 1889. She hoped that it would perform tasks that "none but a woman could do," that required "the fine sensibilities that characterize the true woman."[18] In her own county, where Mayo's influence worked most directly, women's committees decorated Grange halls, held fund-raising socials, and performed various "acts of charity," especially for a hospital in Battle Creek. Mayo disliked telling local committees in other parts of the state what they should do but strongly suggested that they help the poor, even poor city people whose problems had never concerned agricultural organizations before.[19]

Woman's work floundered in most of Michigan until 1893. In 1891, the state committee sponsored a speaking contest that attracted very limited participation. The committee had no definite project in 1892, when Mary Mayo explained that she had given it little attention that year because her daughter's illness had required a long stay in Kansas. Mayo's leadership was, and would remain, absolutely essential to the committee's success. Her trip west at least produced a *Grange Visitor* piece on the good work that the Women's Christian Association was doing for unfortunate women and children in Chicago, and another about the WCTU temple in Evanston. The building stirred her enthusiasm for the proposed Grange temple in Washington. The National Grange had asked woman's work committees to raise money for the project, but little came of the effort, despite Mayo's strong support.[20]

Michigan's state committee began in 1893 with determination and some definite ideas. It urged masters of local Granges to appoint committees—"not half" had yet done so—and charged the committees to visit their neighborhood schools. The visitors were to fill out standard evaluation forms provided by the state Superintendent of Public Instruction. The state committee also asked women to attend local school meetings. Michigan law allowed women to vote in those meetings; the committee urged them to exercise their franchises, in a "ladylike manner," to improve the schools, which meant raising the moral tone of education. Mary Mayo thought, for example, that rhetoric exercises should be made to serve high didactic purposes. Later, in 1896, another member of the committee, who shared Mayo's strong interest in schools, urged that they work to inculcate patriotism. Mary Sherwood Hinds saw an especially urgent need to have immigrant children taught to love the American flag. That became Hinds' special branch of woman's work.

Mayo approved of it and even urged that her colleague's report on patriotism in the schools be read at least once a quarter in every Michigan Grange.[21]

The 1893 committee also published, as a way of making suggestions to inactive sisters, a list of projects that had been carried out by especially vigorous local committees. One local committee, for example, had organized a juvenile Grange. Mayo particularly applauded that and children's day activities. Several committees had raised money by quilting and holding socials. Others had staged historical pageants on Columbus Day, and a few local committees had temperance meetings just before their communities voted on local option prohibition. Michigan's woman's work committees battled the demon rum with persistence and apparent unanimity through the remainder of Mayo's Grange career. The cause brought Grangers into cooperation with other groups of morally advanced women, notably the WCTU.[22]

Charitable activities had the same effect. Mayo knew the women who supported Battle Creek's charity hospital, which received gifts of butter and eggs from Grange farms, and had correspondence with others who sponsored an orphan asylum in Detroit. In 1890, her city contacts suggested that Grange women help Detroit orphans by providing a summer month of farm hospitality. Mayo transmitted that suggestion through the *Grange Visitor*, urging women to receive "these little ones who have never played upon God's green grass."[23] Not much was actually done for such unfortunates until she returned to the idea in 1894. Then Mayo suggested that not only orphans, but also "tired working girls," needed a respite from city life. Urban charities, especially in Detroit, were prepared to pay travel expenses; farm families were merely asked to set an extra place for two summer weeks. Times were hard for farmers in 1894, Mayo knew, but she thought that many of them could afford a little charity.[24]

Her proposal brought some encouraging responses from Grange women, but it also raised questions. Would city visitors be dirty and diseased? "Probably not," Mayo answered; they were supposed to be inspected by physicians before coming. Would they be "obedient and moral?" Most would be, Mayo hoped, but they would "need attention, care, and love, just *mothering*—and we all know what that means."[25] It likely meant more than just setting an extra place; to Mayo, it certainly meant that the fresh air project was an appropriate part of woman's work.

The project met some bitter opposition. One Grange indignantly voted not to participate because, as one of its women wrote, farm people had enough work in the summer without taking additional pains for "these city bummers."[26] Mayo replied that the work was voluntary and that women who thought it unduly burdensome had no obligation to participate. She had taken two working girls into her own home early in the summer of 1894, welcomed a boy soon after they left, and planned to have two more girls a little later. Such visitors had been coming to the Mayo home for "years" before the woman's work committee formally adopted the fresh air project. They were no burden to her, but other women were free not to participate. Mayo simply asked that they forego uncharitable remarks about "city bummers," while considering the possibility that some women who thought themselves overworked lost more energy through "scolding, fretting, and grumbling" than through actual labor.[27]

The fresh air project flourished. In 1898, Kenyon Butterfield, a distinguished authority on rural society who edited the *Grange Visitor* when the project began, identified it as the single most successful woman's work effort anywhere in the Grange. Fifty-one city people had country outings in 1894, and the number increased through the next several years. Butterfield cited Mayo's 1897 report, which said that 707 visitors had taken part in the program through its first four years and that farmers had adopted eighteen city children.[28] Butterfield also suggested, several years earlier, that the project might have other benefits as well. It acquainted city people, notably the prominent leaders of charities, with Grangers and brought Grangers "into contact with the sufferings of other classes." That should have been instructive for both urban and rural participants. Since the Grange was supposed to be educational, the fresh air project was appropriate Grange work, even though it had nothing directly to do with agriculture.[29] Mary Mayo took Butterfield's point a little further. The Grange, she suggested, had begun with a narrow interest in helping farmers. Then the fresh air work gave farmers a chance to help other people. That was morally improving for farmers and would surely increase city dwellers' respect for them.[30]

The National Grange surveyed woman's work throughout the country in 1892. Twenty-six states, mostly in the eastern and midwestern regions where the Order then had three-fifths of its members, submitted brief reports. Only nine western and southern states reported, and only five of them claimed to have active women's work committees. Granges in the west and south were mostly too weak to sustain much activity of any kind, for either gender. The Texas report said as much, pleading that the Grange was at "a very low ebb there," and the Virginia report admitted that the death of one sister had been enough to stop its woman's work committee. In some well-organized western states, however, sisters chose not to commit themselves to woman's work because, as a Colorado woman reported, they preferred to "work shoulder to shoulder with the brothers." Similarly, Californians argued that woman's work could not be separated from other Grange activities. Flora Kimball had told the California State Grange a year earlier that encouraging women to "work in special lines" would make sense only if men were also asked to develop specialties. "Men's Work in the Grange," as she titled her paper on the subject, might include giving business advice to widows who had never learned to manage their own affairs.[31] Such equalitarian feeling in some places, and organizational weakness in others, stifled woman's work outside of the east and midwest. In contrast, of the nine reporting eastern states, only Rhode Island had failed to organize a woman's work committee by 1892. Of the eight reporting midwestern states, only Nebraska had failed to conduct some kind of woman's work, and it had a committee that claimed to favor the idea.[32]

The twenty states that reported specific activities had broadly similar ideas of woman's work, though a few reported distinctive projects. Eleven of the twenty said that the sisters were contributing to programs; seven said that they were managing juvenile activities; six mentioned some effort, usually unsuccessful, to raise money for the National Grange temple in Washington; and three claimed to have raised money for Grange halls, or to have decorated existing halls. A few had organized charitable activities. Illinois and Iowa sisters had raised money for flood victims; New Yorkers had done the same for starving Russian peasants, for which they received thanks from Count Leo Tolstoi. New Yorkers, like their Michigan sisters, had also contributed to hospitals and participated in a fresh air program.[33]

Some women's work committees engaged in other kinds of social uplift. Only two state committees mentioned temperance work in their reports to the national committee in 1892, but others certainly gave it major emphasis. The Michigan, Massachusetts, Delaware, New York, and Wisconsin committees all stressed temperance in reporting to their state Granges, and several state committees worked to improve education. The Mississippi committee, an exception to the general absence of woman's work in the south, was especially active in that area. It fostered school construction and created a training institute for teachers to attend when their schools were out. The committee implied that Grange women did much of the work connected with those institutes, though it did not claim exclusive jurisdiction over them.[34]

On the evidence of the 1892 reports, woman's work covered a lot of territory. Unlike other committees, which had fairly definite responsibilities, woman's work could be anything that interested women. Because its definition was so broad, it was difficult to distinguish from the duties that belonged to Grange women acting in other capacities or to Grange men. That produced a great deal of soul-searching about whether the committees should continue. The two members of New Hampshire's committee struggled with the question in 1893, concluding that men and women did the same work in the Grange but "there is a subtle line of difference" that justified the committee's existence. The line was too subtle for the committee to draw, but the members sensed its importance.[35] Eliza Gifford offered a stronger defense of woman's work in 1891. Its charge seemed vague and had confused some women, but the Order needed a committee that encouraged women's participation. Before the woman's work committees began, some women had participated fully, but the "mass of women members" had not. The committees were "indispensable" because they recognized and encouraged women more effectively than anything that the Grange had done before.[36]

Apparently, most of the women who attended the 1893 National Grange considered the committees, or at least their national capstone, something less than indispensable. A Colorado sister, who had told the 1892 National Grange that she objected to a separate women's committee on principle, proposed that the national committee be discontinued and that states be allowed to continue or discontinue their committees as they pleased. The National Grange passed her motion after it had been endorsed by a separate vote of the women members.[37] It freed states that had never been able to sustain woman's work committees, or had chosen not to do so, from having to file empty or negative reports. Some other states, where woman's work had been more successful, also eliminated their committees but continued aspects of woman's work under other rubrics. The Ohio State Grange, for example, promptly abolished its woman's work committee and gave the time that had been occupied by its reports to sisters who read papers about farm women's drudgery and their right to be treated as partners in their farm businesses.[38] After the Illinois State Grange dropped its committee, women members concentrated on the education committee, which became a vehicle for their interests in kindergartens, temperance, and the veneration of "great women," particularly Harriet Beecher Stowe and Francis Willard.[39] Indiana women also turned to their education committee when woman's work was discontinued. Their 1893 education report concerned equal suffrage, which they strongly favored, and alcohol, narcotics, indecent literature, and patent monopolies, all of which they opposed. They also observed that cities received too much of the state school fund, but their report did not dwell on schools.[40] Education, as the Illinois and Indiana committees defined it, was much broader than schools. It was about as broad as woman's work.

Other states maintained woman's work committees long after their national capstone had been removed. Massachusetts, which originated the idea, kept its committee until the turn of the century. The 1894 Massachusetts report was a simple list of tasks that women performed in their Granges but said nothing about activities undertaken by the special women's committee. Later reports exhorted women to perform the same domestic tasks in the Grange that they carried out at home and to seize the educational opportunities that the Grange provided.[41]

One of their principal home tasks was child care, which the chairman of the New York State Grange woman's work committee thought was "one of the most natural lines" in which her committee could work. If women looked after children during Grange meetings, she suggested, attendance would improve and children would learn to love the Order.[42] Similarly, the Oregon committee reported no concrete actions but used its place on the 1897 program to call for equal suffrage and celebrate women's expanding vocational opportunities.[43] The somewhat more ambitious New Jersey committee supplemented the state Lecturer's work by suggesting topics for discussion in local Granges. In 1902, for example, the New Jersey committee asked Granges to consider topics including roses, schools, and climate. A few New Jersey Granges devoted a meeting to some woman's work topic each month, but the state Master complained in 1903 that many subordinate Granges did not have woman's work committees to arrange the discussions and that Lecturers too often ignored the suggested topics.[44] The Kansas woman's work committee, which revived in 1906, proposed topics as late as 1914. Suggestions for that year included Kansas women's readiness for the franchise, the benefits farm women would derive from voting, sterilization as a punishment for sex crimes, whether mothers were competent teachers of sex hygiene, and books on sex that might be useful to mothers.[45] Rhode Island women, who had been slow to organize their woman's work committee, sustained it long after its counterparts had disappeared from most other states. The Rhode Island committee exhorted women to visit absent members, help their Lecturers and graces, decorate their halls, and encourage children's participation. Later, in the 1910s, it advocated equal suffrage and prohibition; its chairman represented the Grange on the legislative committee of the state's Woman Suffrage Association.[46] Similarly, Michigan's 1910 woman's work committee asked members to visit schools, try to get kindergartens and nature study programs into rural schools, encourage temperance and good morals generally, and work to preserve "bits of beauty for public parks." It continued to advocate preservation in 1911, when it also recommended that court houses have "rest rooms" where rural woman could relax, eat their lunches, or hold meetings when they came to town.[47]

State and local woman's work committees did not all disappear when the national committee disbanded, but they often yielded to other ways of organizing Grange women. Active sisters took control of education committees, organized juvenile Granges, and formed local "ladies' aid" groups. Some of the last began while woman's work committees were still new. At least one Pennsylvania Grange had a ladies' aid in 1889, and the women of La Prairie Grange in Wisconsin organized a similar "ladies' mutual benefit society" in 1890. The Wisconsin group met every two weeks to help families through emergencies and to make quilts, which it auctioned to raise money for charitable projects. And it began a little fair, also as a fund-raising project, in 1895. Gradually becoming "just a social card playing club," the society survived in that form for at least eighty years.[48] Similarly, the women of Honey Creek Grange in Vigo County, Indiana, organized a "Grange sewing circle" in 1900 to raise money for a piano and various improvements to their hall.[49] A decade later, Jennie Buell observed ladies' aids in Michigan Granges; she thought they were a new development, which suggests that their predecessors were little known beyond their immediate neighborhoods. The Michigan ladies' aids usually met for "two or three hours of work" followed by supper and sociability before regular Grange meetings. The women enjoyed each others' company while decorating their Grange halls and preparing food.[50] A Michigan sister praised her ladies' aid in a 1917 poem for decorating its hall and raising money to pay Grange debts. She thought that it was indispensable.[51] But most Granges apparently got along without organized ladies' aids, although women in many places worked together informally for the Order's and each others' good. The sisters of Big Creek Grange in Warren County, Missouri, for example, held their own special meetings at a member's home to finish quilts that their hostess had never found time to assemble. She had been an active Granger for twenty-five years, had raised twelve children, and her friends thought that she deserved a little help.[52]

Ladies' aids, like woman's work committees, tried to meet the persistently felt need for Grange organizations in which women could work with their sisters in their distinctive interests. Elizabeth Patterson, Ceres of the National Grange, initiated a much more general and enduring effort to meet that need in 1910. The home economics committee that the National Grange then created became a permanent part of the Order. Its name changed to women's activities department in 1967, but it has operated continuously from 1910 to the present. Initially more clearly focused than the woman's work committees had been, it set out to encourage the systematic study of domestic work.

Thoughtful domesticity was a well-established Grange interest that Patterson promoted for several years before the committee's inception, while she was Ceres of the National Grange, by editing the "Grange Home Department" of the *National Grange* magazine. Domestic features in Grange journals had previously been narrowly practical or inspirational; they told women to make their homes beautiful, in order to beautify their families' souls, or to put springs on kitchen doors to keep flies out. Hoping to encourage more rigorous thinking, Patterson selected a technical essay on dietetics, with a table showing the protein and calories in various foods, for one installment of the "Home Department" and a piece on bacteria in milk for another. The milk report credited research done at Cornell and advised women to read a bulletin from the same institution. Married to a chemist who headed Maryland's experiment station and served as acting President of its university, Patterson respected academic science.[53] She told the 1909 National Grange that its useful lessons should be taught to rural homemakers. Everything except cooking and housekeeping had benefited from science, she argued, while women continued to plod along in their mothers' footsteps. She wanted them to read and ask new questions. For example, rather than settling for food that tasted good, they should ask if they had spent their money "so as to get the most and best nourishment for it?" Ultimately, as she had learned from the famous home economist Ellen H. Richards, scientific knowledge would allow homemakers to simplify their work and free themselves "for the more important and permanent interests of the home and of society." Home economics, therefore, had the broad significance that Grange women had long claimed for domesticity.[54]

The national home economics committee, which Patterson headed for several years, departed from the precedent of woman's work in one respect and followed it in others. Unlike woman's work, it focused at first on a fairly specific topic rather than a gender. Its first five members included two men, and men served on the committee through 1918 when they were three of its six members. In 1919, and in every year thereafter, only women served on the committee.[55] Like the woman's work committee, it operated through state committees, which in turn fostered home economics work in local Granges. The national committee enunciated broad purposes, exhorted its state and local counterparts, and reported on their accomplishments.

The national committee's first report, in 1911, began by defining home economics as comprehending everything "that touches home life, the structure of the house, its furnishings, equipment, management and sanitary care, the care and training of the children, the purchase and preparation of the food," and every other aspect of homemaking. The scientific study of such matters, the committee observed, was fairly new. It recognized that the University of Illinois had offered a home economics course long before, but the study had only recently, in part because of efforts by women's clubs, spread into many agricultural colleges and other schools. In 1911, the committee enthused, home economics was flourishing. Granges could make it part of their programs by studying the "Home Progress" course then being published by Houghton Mifflin and by getting other publications and expert speakers from state colleges. The committee urged Lecturers, graces, and local home economics committees to make full use of those resources.[56]

In 1912, the committee got an indication of how Granges had responded to the national home economics initiative. Questionnaires, returned by eighteen of the twenty-nine state Granges, reported that three of them were making ambitious efforts to teach home economics to their members, twelve had given some support to the Page-Wilson bill that provided federal money for vocational education including home economics, eight had home economics committees, and three state Masters intended to appoint such committees at their next meetings. Ten reported that they were cooperating in unspecified ways with home economics teachers at their state colleges; in "some instances," home economics faculty members were personally active in the Granges. Finally, some of them asked the national home economics committee to provide outlines and reading lists, and one state Lecturer asked for an explanation of what college home economics departments could be expected to do for rural women.

The committee responded to the last request by reporting that some of the better college home economics departments provided three-month and even one-week short courses, conducted summer schools for teachers, published "Reading Courses for Farmers' Wives" and other instructive bulletins, and judged at fairs. The committee particularly hoped that the home economists' participation in fairs would make women's competitions more instructive than they generally had been. Fairs, the committee opined, had lavished too much attention on old-fashioned crafts, such as patchwork quilting, which were of "no value to the modern housewife." Home economists, the committee hoped, would get fairs to emphasize canning, which preserved the flavor and nutritional value of fruits and vegetables.[57]

The committee continued in that vein until World War I. It tried to bring Grange women into contact with academic home economists who offered a modern, scientific approach to housekeeping, which was expected to lighten women's work and make housekeeping a "profession."[58] The committee also applauded the extension workers who appeared throughout the country after 1914. They carried home economics to women outside the Grange and to girls who joined canning clubs and other precursors of the 4-H movement. Within a decade, an historian has argued, extension agents and their new organizations, 4-H and the Farm Bureau, deprived the Grange of some functions and much support. But the enthusiastic 1915 and 1916 home economics reports did not anticipate that result. They viewed extension, like the college home economics departments themselves, as a simple blessing.[59]

The committee's emphasis changed slightly when the United States went to war in 1917. It still advocated scientific housekeeping but focused very specifically on preventing waste, especially of food. The federal government, which meant to conserve resources for its own martial purposes, had urged women to use food with patriotic efficiency, and the committee loyally answered the call.[60] The committee continued that emphasis in 1918, when it also reported that state and local home economics committees had found various ways to support the Red Cross, and criticized Herbert Hoover's Food Administration for not sufficiently involving rural women in food conservation efforts. In addition, the committee condemned the government for encouraging cigarette smoking among soldiers, lamented the decline of rural hospitality, and asked the National Grange to provide $1,000 for the committee's work. The committee got its money. The appropriation strengthened it only slightly but started home economics on the way to becoming a well-financed and consistently active part of the Order. And the committee's laments about smoking and rural hospitality signaled another change. The focus of home economics had broadened to include the moral and social interests of the earlier woman's work committees.[61] The committee continued to take a broad view of its charge in 1919, when it again lamented that the cigarette habit, which was as bad as drinking, had been "fastened upon the country during the war." One form of intemperance had ended, legally, but another had taken its place. The committee also urged people to remember the habits of thrift that the war had encouraged, to be sure that children got enough animal foods despite their rising cost, and to resist the "extravagance and immodesty" then fashionable in women's clothing.[62]

By that time, home economics committees, like the preceding woman's work committees, had become vehicles for Grange women's various causes. Unlike their predecessors, the home economics committees began with a fairly narrow, domestic definition of their subject. They soon cast a wider net, just as their predecessors had done, but the scientific study of homemaking remained at the core of their interest. The committee's leaders thought that home economics could liberate women from mindless drudgery. From their very beginning, Grangers had said that drudgery was the greatest problem in farm women's lives. Finally, in the first few years of the twentieth century, they had found its solution.

NOTES

1. *Proceedings of the Fourth Annual Session of the Indiana State Grange* (Indianapolis: State Grange, 1874), 32.

2. Grosh, *Mentor in the Granges and Homes of Patrons of Husbandry*, 388.

3. *Journal of Proceedings of the Fourteenth Annual Session of the National Grange of the Patrons of Husbandry*, 1880, committee reports.

4. Minutes of Olive Grange No. 189 for January 28, 1888, in Indiana Historical Society.

5. Smith, *The History of the Iowa State Grange*, 5–6.

6. *Journal of Proceedings of the Thirty-Third Session of the National Grange of the Patrons of Husbandry*, 1899, 6–9.

7. *Record of Proceedings of the Thirteenth Annual Session of the Massachusetts State Grange* (Worcester: State Grange, 1885), 60–64.

8. Amelia J. Fuller, "What the Grange has done for Women, and Women for the Grange" in *The Connecticut Granges* (New Haven: Industrial Publishing Co., 1900), 419.

9. *Record of Proceedings of the Fifteenth Annual Session of the Massachusetts State Grange*, 1888, 11, 96–97.

10. *Journal of Proceedings of the Twenty-Second Session of the National Grange*, 1888, 107.

11. *Journal of Proceedings of the Twenty-Third Session of the National Grange*, 1889, 118.

12. *Journal of Proceedings of the Sixth Annual Session of the Rhode Island State Grange, Patrons of Husbandry, 1893* (Pascoag: State Grange, 1893), 66–67.

13. *Journal of Proceedings of the Seventh Annual Session of the Rhode Island State Grange, Patrons of Husbandry*, 1894, Master's report.

14. *Twentieth Session of the Iowa State Grange*, 1889, 10.

15. *Journal of Proceedings of the Twenty-First Session of the Iowa State Grange*, 1890, 18–19.

16. *Twenty-First Annual Session of the Indiana State Grange*, 1892, 9.

17. *Journal of Proceedings of the Eighteenth Annual Session of the Ohio State Grange*, 1890, 33; *National Grange Monthly* 15 (February 1918): 7; Gardner, *The Grange*, 213.

18. Buell, *One Woman's Work*, 43.

19. *Grange Visitor* 15 (15 December 1890): 4.

20. Ibid. 16 (1 October 1981): 1; 17 (1 June 1892): 6; (1 August 1982): 6.

21. Ibid. 18 (1 February 1893): 5; 19 (20 December 1894): 5; 21 (16 January 1896): 3, 5; (2 April 1896): 3.

22. Ibid. 18 (1 January 1893): 6.

23. Ibid.; 19 (17 May 1894): 3; 15 (15 December 1890): 4; Walter S. Ufford, *Fresh Air Charity in the United States* (New York: Bonnell, Silver and Co., 1897).

24. *Grange Visitor* 19 (3 May 1894): 3.

25. Ibid. 19 (7 June 1894): 3.

26. Ibid. 19 (July 1894): 3; (6 September 1894): 3.

27. Ibid. 19 (2 August 1894): 3.

28. Kenyon Butterfield, "Recent Grange Work in Michigan," *The Outlook* 60 (17 September 1898): 176–79.

29. *Grange Visitor* 20 (15 August 1895): 3.

30. Ibid. 20 (15 August 1895): 3.

31. *Journal of Proceedings of the Nineteenth Annual Session of the California State Grange 1891* (San Francisco: State Grange, 1891): 76–79.

32. *Journal of Proceedings of the Twenty-Sixth Session of the National Grange*, 1892, 155–63.

33. Ibid.

34. Ibid.; *Journal of Proceedings of the Twenty-Second Annual Session of the Massachusetts State Grange*, 1894, 66–69; *Journal of Proceedings of the Eighteenth Annual Session of the Delaware State Grange 1892* (Wilmington: State Grange, 1892), 20–22; *Journal of Proceedings of the Eighteenth Annual Session of the New York State Grange 1891* (Elmira: State Grange, 1891), 111–14; *Journal of Proceedings of the*

Twenty-Second Annual Session of the Wisconsin State Grange, 1892, 22–25; *Grange Visitor* 18 (1 January 1893): 6.

35. *Journal of Proceedings of the Twentieth Annual Session of the New Hampshire State Grange*, 1893, 91–93.

36. *The Husbandman* 18 (25 November 1891): 1.

37. Gardner, *The Grange*, 203–4.

38. *Journal of Proceedings of the Twenty-First Annual Session of the Ohio State Grange*, 1893, 65–70.

39. *Journal of Proceedings of the Twenty-Third Annual Session of the Illinois State Grange 1894* (Peoria: State Grange, 1894), 22, 41–42; *Journal of Proceedings of the Twenty-Fourth Session of the Illinois State Grange*, 1895, 40–42.

40. *Journal of Proceedings of the Twenty-Third Annual Session of the Indiana State Grange*, 1893, 25, 36.

41. *Journal of Proceedings of the Twenty-Second Annual Session of the Massachusetts State Grange*, 1894, 66–69; *Twenty-Third Annual Session*, 1895, 65–66; *Twenty Fourth Annual Session*, 1896, 70.

42. *Pennsylvania Grange News* 2 (August 1905): 7–8.

43. *Journal of Proceedings of the Twenty-Fourth Annual Session of the Oregon State Grange 1897* (Woodburn: State Grange, 1897), 50–53.

44. *Journal of Proceedings of the Thirtieth Annual Session of the State Grange of New Jersey*, 1902, 73–74; *Thirty-First Annual Session*, 1903, 23.

45. *National Grange Monthly* 11 (June 1914): 9.

46. *Journal of Proceedings of the Nineteenth Annual Session of the Rhode Island State Grange, Patrons of Husbandry*, 1905, 35–36; *Twenty-First Annual Session*, 1907, 25–27; Janet Hopkins, *History of Rhode Island State Grange* (N.p.: State Grange, 1939), 39.

47. *National Grange* 6 (11 May 1910): 10; *National Grange Monthly* 8 (July 1911): 3.

48. Laverne H. Marquart, *Wisconsin's Agricultural Heritage: The Grange, 1871–1971* (Lake Mills: Rural Life Publishing Co., 1972), 87–88.

49. *American Grange Bulletin and Scientific Farmer* 33 (15 October 1903): 10.

50. *National Grange Monthly* 8 (August 1911): 6; *Farmer's Friend and Grange Advocate* 19 (2 January 1892): 1; *American Grange Bulletin and Scientific Farmer* 33 (15 October 1903): 10.

51. *Michigan Patron* 16 (August 1917): 3.

52. *American Grange Bulletin and Scientific Farmer* 26 (29 June 1899): 1.

53. Leonard, *Woman's Who's Who of America*, 626; *National Grange* 3 (23 December 1908): 8.

54. *National Grange* 3 (24 March 1909): 6; 4 (13 October 1909): 12–13; 5 (8 December 1909): 10–11; (15 December 1909): 11.

55. See reports of the home economics chairmen in the National Grange *Proceedings*, especially *Journal of Proceedings of the National Grange of the Patrons of Husbandry Fifty-Second Annual Session*, 1918, 161–63 and *Fifty-Third Annual Session*, 1919, 170–72.

56. *Journal of Proceedings of the Forty-Fifth Annual Session of the National Grange*, 1911, 139–41.

57. *Journal of Proceedings of the National Grange of the Patrons of Husbandry Forty-Sixth Annual Session*, 1912, 88–95; Matthews, *"Just a Housewife"*, 112, 146, re-

peatedly criticizes home economists for devaluing women's craft traditions. The Grange home economics committee's disparagement of quilting illustrates her point.

58. *Journal of Proceedings of the Forty-Sixth Annual Session of the National Grange,* 1913, 157.

59. *Journal of Proceedings of the National Grange of the Patrons of Husbandry Forty-Ninth Annual Session,* 1915, 127–29; *Fiftieth Annual Session,* 1916, 154–56; William D. Barns, *The West Virginia State Grange: The First Century 1873–1973* (Morgantown: Morgantown Printing and Binding Co., 1973), 156–58.

60. *Journal of Proceedings of the National Grange of the Patrons of Husbandry Fifty-First Annual Session,* 1917, 196.

61. *Journal of Proceedings of the National Grange of the Patrons of Husbandry Fifty-Second Annual Session,* 1918, 161–63.

62. *Journal of Proceedings of the National Grange of the Patrons of Husbandry Fifty-Third Annual Session,* 1919, 170–72.

6

The "World's Greatest Equality Club"

Dennis Sven Nordin's valuable history of the Grange reports that "the order never wavered on the question of extending suffrage and equal rights to the fairer sex."[1] In fact, the earliest Grange positions on equal suffrage were cautious, negative, or downright hostile. Within a few years, however, women and a few men began using Grange forums to demand votes for women. Then caution and opposition gradually turned to support. The Order's receptiveness to their efforts may have owed something to its huge membership losses in the late 1870s; historians who describe the passage of equal suffrage resolutions in the California and Iowa State Granges both suggest that members took increased interest in women and their causes in order to win favorable publicity and new women members. The fact that support for equal suffrage was growing in the country at large, and that suffragists were giving increasing weight to arguments that were consistent with conventional ideas about women's domestic responsibilities, must surely have encouraged Grangers to support equal suffrage, too.[2]

Whatever their motives, Grangers soon opened their programs and publications to women who argued that equal suffrage was a natural right, a potentially decisive weapon against alcohol, and a logical implication of the Order's frequent promises to treat women as equals.[3] Then spirited debates produced a long series of resolutions favoring equal suffrage. There is little reason to think that the resolutions had any practical importance, but the debates inspired some of Grange women's most serious efforts and kept women's rights on the Order's agendas, at least intermittently, for more than forty years.

The earliest Grangers got embroiled in the equal suffrage debates as an indirect and unintended result of accepting women members and publishing a great deal of respectful rhetoric about women's value to the organization. Later Grangers took pride in their founders' equalitarian professions, but some organizers in the early 1870s feared that they might repel potential members by raising the spectre of "woman's rights." D. Wyatt Aiken, for example, who was the principal Grange organizer in South Carolina, thought that he had to propitiate suspicious conservatives. "But you admit women," he paraphrased them; does that mean that "you advocate woman's rights?" Aiken assured them that it did not. The Grange barred all discussion of political and religious topics and, therefore, could not endorse women's rights. It included women members in order to enhance the Order's "social worth" and to give widows who were trying to operate farms on their own a circle of helpful friends; he thought that the second justification had particular force in the *post bellum* south, though he later guessed that his assurances had been futile, that women's presence in the Order had contributed to its unpopularity in his region.[4] William Simmons, another South Carolina organizer, rejected any Grange connection with women's rights agitation far more vehemently than did Aiken. He recognized that the "woman membership feature. . . . appeared to be a very objectionable one." Critics argued that women who left their homes to join organizations such as the Grange were well on their way to "woman's rights." But Simmons answered that women could join the Grange without any such danger. After all, "the woman's rights movement is a political abortion, (conceived in the diseased brains of a few dissolute women, the mere mention of any connection with which would bring the blush of shame to every pure woman's cheek,) while at the Grange all political discussions are rigorously prohibited." Moreover, women were safe in the Grange because they attended with their husbands and brothers. It was a family, not a women's organization.[5]

Grangers offered similar assurances outside of the south, too. The National Grange published the Aiken and Simmons statements as recruiting leaflets; Oliver Hudson Kelley appended a membership appeal to Simmons' statement, as he did to a similar publication by a Vermont organizer. Trying to conciliate a brother who feared that "if women were allowed a part in running the organization, pretty soon some fool would advocate that they vote in general elections," the Vermont writer declared that "I do not believe in woman suffrage, nor never can." He hoped that women's participation in the Grange would simply encourage them to improve in their "sphere" and stimulate men to "highminded action."[6] Another northern leader, A. B. Smedley, who was Master of the Iowa State Grange in 1874, said that the Order had embraced "women's rights" only if that meant working "in harmony with . . . wives, daughters, and sisters." Grangers simply wanted to help overworked farm women, which was not in the least subversive.[7] Similarly, the *Pacific Rural Press*, which strongly supported California's Grange movement, reported in 1874 that the Grange had been criticized for its "supposed sympathy" with women's suffrage but denied that it had any special affinity for the cause.[8] And the Maryland State Grange offered the same assurance at its 1874 organizational meeting. It promised not to be "a woman's rights association or a place for strong minded women."[9]

Some Grange women also expressed caution about changing their civil status. For example, an Ohio woman assured her state Grange in 1876 that she disagreed with "those of the fairer sex who seem to wish to enter the arena of life as man's peers," but she insisted that women deserved respect and encouragement within their "proper sphere." Their sphere, she was glad to say, included the Grange.[10] A Trempeleau County, Wisconsin, woman disavowed political ambition somewhat less reassuringly. She was "no advocate of 'Woman Suffrage,' " she wrote, because nothing could be gained by letting women vote until they were fully informed about public questions. Then she urged her sisters to study politics as much as their work permitted and argue for their opinions "with as much assurance and independence as our 'Liege Lords.' " The Wisconsin sister had already studied enough to develop one strong political opinion: President Hayes stood for "purity" and had given a thoroughly sound inaugural address.[11] She denied that she was a suffragist, but her essay implied that conservatives were right to worry about Grange women's aspirations.

The National Grange offered a cautious statement of its official doctrine about women in 1874 as part of the Declaration of Purposes to which the Order still adheres. The Declaration calls for independence of middlemen, an end to divisive sectionalism, and improved education. It also endorses domestic science in agricultural colleges, more comfortable and attractive farm homes, and "a proper appreciation of the abilities and sphere of woman, as is indicated by admitting her to membership in our Order." Grange advocates of equal suffrage later invoked that "appreciation" to considerable persuasive effect, but nothing in the Declaration gives them explicit support. It emphasizes women's sphere but says nothing of women's rights.[12]

The Reverend Aaron Grosh explained Grange ideas about women more fully, and at least as cautiously, in his 1876 book *Mentor in the Granges and Homes of Patrons of Husbandry*. Grosh was the first Chaplain of the National Grange, and his book is a magisterial commentary on the Order's ritual and doctrine. He wrote that women were absolutely essential to the Order and to society in general. Woman's "gentle influence, her innate tact in all matters of good taste and propriety, her instinctive perceptions of righteousness and purity—all these are needed in the Grange, and also in society at large." The Grange was a channel through which women's virtues could be released from "seclusion" into the harsh, masculine world. Their release did not require " 'Woman Suffrage' and 'Woman's Rights.' " Grosh made that very explicit; the first subtitle in his chapter on "Woman in the Grange" is "Not there politically." Hostile critics accused the Grange of fostering political ambitions among its women members, but that simply was not true. The Grange, Grosh accurately reported, had taken no official position on equal suffrage when he published his book. Further, he argued there was no risk that women who were accustomed to voting and leadership in the Grange would try to extend their privileges into public life. There was a clear line between the Grange and politics. The Grange was domestic, an extension of home, not political. Voting in the Grange, therefore, had no more to do with voting for government officials than did "voting for officers or for resolutions in a sewing circle."[13]

Grosh thought that women's place in the Grange was politically innocuous, but men who feared that equality within the Order might spill over into the great world had a point. Grangers began to hear arguments in favor of women's rights in general and equal suffrage in particular within their first decade. In 1874, for example, an Illinois woman expressed pleasure that women outnumbered men at a joint meeting of two subordinate Granges. Grange activity was particularly good for women, she said, because it educated them and made them want the franchise.[14] In the same year, a particularly outspoken Minnesota brother contributed an essay on equal suffrage to Maine's Grange journal, *The Dirigo Rural*. He denied that the Order's ban on political controversy extended to the suffrage; it excluded partisan squabbles but not discussions of issues touching the Order's essential principles. He thought that equality between men and women was an essential principle and that Grange experience had demonstrated how well equal suffrage worked. The practice would be equally beneficial to the government, which would change from "bachelor-hall" to "ladies parlor." Women voters would clean "out the filthy stables of masculine corruption." Two years later, he wrote a similar essay attributing "temperance, peace, and moral virtue" to women, particularly women of the "Caucasian race," while blaming men for warfare.[15]

Other Grangers broached the suffrage issue more guardedly. In 1876, for example, the Master of New Hampshire's state Grange denied that Grangers were "direct advocates of equal suffrage" but suggested that by participating in the Order, "woman may show herself capable of many things heretofore considered, even by most members of her own sex, as entirely unfitted."[16] A year earlier, the Wisconsin State Grange recommended that women be eligible for local school offices, and in 1878, the California State Grange asked its state constitutional convention to enact equal suffrage for all purposes.[17]

California Granges had been identified with women's rights to an extraordinary degree since the *Pacific Rural Press* began to promote the Order in 1871. The paper tried to recruit women by emphasizing the Grangers' equalitarian professions. In 1873, when the California State Grange held its first meeting, the *Press* enthused that it was part of the "step by step, slow but sure" progress of women toward equality. The *Press* also denied that the Order supported equal suffrage, but its very general pronouncements in favor of equality may have helped to attract the committed suffragists who soon magnified the Order's support for women's rights. Concerned that Grange equalitarianism had been exaggerated, John A. Hamilton, Master of the California State Grange, pointed out that the Order had taken no official position on the suffrage question. He also told the organizational meeting of the Delaware State Grange that "we are not admirers of the strong minded who, forgetful of that delicacy and propriety which so endears woman to our hearts, and gives her such a hold upon our affections, would usurp the place for which a kind creator never made them." Then women in his own state Grange met apart from their brothers, heard suffragist oratory, and began the three-year campaign that ended with a clear endorsement of their position. The California State Grange declared for equal suffrage in 1878 and sent members, including Jeanne Carr, to speak for the cause before a committee of the state constitutional convention.[18]

The New York and Indiana state Granges endorsed equal suffrage in 1881. New Yorkers had debated the issue since 1875, when their Ladies' Committee, which included all of the sisters present in the state Grange, issued a report on the status of women in the Order. It began with fervent expressions of gratitude for all that the Grange was doing to broaden women's social and intellectual horizons and then called for expanded "opportunities for woman outside the Grange as well as in."[19] Probably a guarded call for equal suffrage, the report certainly provided the occasion for a closely subsequent flurry of anti-suffrage pronouncements by male Grangers. A local Master, for example, denounced "strong-minded ladies" who sought to "violate" female character by enfranchising women. The Grange, in wholesome contrast to such harpies, was uplifting women in ways that harmonized with their distinctive virtues.[20] Then a writer in *The Husbandman*, journal of the New York State Grange, asserted that overworked farm women, whom he described with palpable sympathy, would get no benefit from voting. That only interested a pampered elite. Confident of his readers' biblical knowledge, he reminded women that "to all men Ruth is the sweetest type of womanhood, and it is their desire to have you remain so forever."[21]

That plea for submissiveness brought a distinctly strong-minded response from Ella C. Goodell of Canastota, New York, whose acerbic and often elegant writing frequently enlivened the journal in the 1870s and early 1880s. She argued from an elastic understanding of women's domestic sphere. Woman, she wrote, should be "the priestess of the home." At the same time, her "broad charity" should "embrace the world and all its duties." Her understanding of women's responsibilities resembled Francis Willard's "home protection" doctrine, which held that women had to act upon the world in order to keep its evils from engulfing their homes, but it was a little simpler and more positive. Her argument may have owed as much to John Ruskin as to Willard. In the second part of his popular *Sesame and Lilies*, Ruskin taught that "woman has a personal work and duty relating to her home, and a public work and duty which is also the expansion of that." *The Husbandman* quoted that passage, accurately and approvingly, a few years later.[22]

Referring directly to the male writer's desire that women be like the biblical Ruth, "the sweetest type of womanhood" and a classic model of self-abnegation, Goodell argued that women were not obliged to be what men desired. Woman was not "made for man, created to minister to his passions and desires." Her place in the world was coordinate to man's and fully equal to it. That closely resembled a sentence from the women's Grange initiation, which said that woman "was intended by her Creator to be neither the slave, the tyrant, nor the toy of man, but to be his helpmeet, his companion, his equal." Finally, Goodell argued that voting really would benefit overworked farm women. It would inspire them to read and think, which would equip them to rise from drudgery to the higher parts of women's sphere.[23]

A little later, Goodell wrote in answer to a woman who had spoken against equal suffrage in the Wayne County Grange Council. The speech, printed in *The Husbandman*, argued that women needed no rights that the "noble, generous" nature of men had not already granted. As for voting, the speaker had three votes—those of her husband and two grown sons. Goodell answered first by suggesting that the three men might "have each a mind of their own." Then she asked who voted for women who owned no franchised citizens. That may have been a little facetious, but Goodell was clearly in earnest when she asserted that prohibition could never be enacted by male votes alone. Temperance required equal suffrage, just as Francis Willard said.[24]

A lively argument followed that exchange. The woman with three votes answered that men should not have minds of their own where moral issues are at stake. She would never "consent that my husband or sons should be on the wrong side, neither would I rest until their convictions coincided with my own."[25] Her certainty that she could shape their opinions illustrated the common view that women's existing influence was stronger than their votes could be. Other New York women advanced the even more common idea that voting would taint female purity. One conceded that women's votes might be needed to win prohibition and that laws in general would be better if women had a hand in making them. But still she insisted that the cost to women themselves would be excessive. The only way to work for temperance without sacrificing purity was to pray for it.[26]

The anti-suffrage views expressed in New York persisted among Grangers all over the country long after the Order went on record in favor of equal suffrage. But the Order did go on record, at various times in various units, because women kept the issue constantly on Grange agendas. They persistently argued that women should not be taxed without representation, that they were at least as capable of civic participation as men, that voting would enliven women's minds by encouraging them to think about public issues, that women's suffrage was a necessary step toward prohibition, and that the Order's professions about women, properly understood, implied a commitment to equal suffrage.

The argument that prohibition required equal suffrage invoked an important Grange commitment. In 1883, for example, the Michigan State Grange called temperance "one of the essential principles upon which our Order is founded," criticized its state legislature for not enacting prohibition, and showed so much interest in the topic that a member thought that it could have been taken for a meeting of Good Templars.[27] That confusion was even more likely in Minnesota, where a unit of the temperance order met in a Grange Hall, sometimes jointly with the Grangers themselves, and then returned the favor by making its Minneapolis hall available for Grange assemblies.[28] Relations between Grangers and the WCTU were at least equally close. The Poplar Ridge, New York, woman who observed of her Grange that "nearly all the ladies are also W.C.T.U.s" probably described a common situation.[29] An Illinois state official may have exaggerated when he complained that "these d-d Grangers are all prohibitionists," but not by much.[30]

Sarah C. Carpenter of Rhode Island linked suffrage to temperance and other moral reforms with special vehemence. Carpenter was Chaplain of the Rhode Island State Grange for a decade after its foundation in 1887 and used her place on state Grange programs to urge the members to work for moral reforms. When another Grange woman told her that the Grange was "not a reform institution," Carpenter replied that if it was not, "then I with many other older sisters and some brothers are in a large degree wasting our time in working for it."[31] In 1893, Carpenter opined that "the worst element of the nation seems to be ruling now" and casting its votes for liquor. The worst were immigrants, slum dwellers, anarchists, southern blacks, and Indians. At the same time, "half of the citizens, the best educated, the most Christian, the most moral portion of the population, and two-thirds of the members of all the churches are disfranchised." She meant women, who would vote "under the leadership of Francis Willard" for education, social

purity, and temperance. To assure that the best women voted, along
with the best men, she proposed that all voters meet the same "educational test."[32]

Grange women also based a persistent argument on the Order's 1874
Declaration of Purposes and its other laudatory words about women
and their sphere. By regularly defining that sphere as including some
kind of social outreach, women were able to argue that the Order's
commitment to them implied support for equal suffrage. Eliza Gifford,
one of the most persistent equal suffrage advocates in the Grange, recalled in 1894 that the "prejudice of ignorance" at first kept Grangers
from understanding that they had committed themselves to votes for
women, but logical explication of Grange principles forced them to the
right conclusion.[33] Of course, the women who made that explication
had to ignore the early Grangers' careful distinction of their sort of
equality from the inappropriate kind demanded by women's rights advocates, but they did that persuasively enough to get equal suffrage
resolutions through various Granges.

Eliza Gifford barely got one of those resolutions passed by the New
York State Grange meeting of 1881. Declaring that the fundamental
Grange principle of equality required equal suffrage, it won "only by
the vote of the presiding officer." Many New York State Grange members voted against Gifford's resolution on the grounds that voting and
fighting should go together and that only bad women would want to
vote anyway.[34] But the number of dissenters shrank in subsequent
years when similar resolutions passed more easily. In 1893, when a
convention met to revise the state constitution, the Grange asked its
members to vote for convention delegates who favored equal suffrage
and instructed its woman's work committee to distribute petitions favoring the reform.[35]

The Indiana State Grange also passed a resolution favoring equal suffrage in 1881. It came to the floor immediately after the Lecturer, Sallie
J. Back, offered a resolution that urged members to support candidates
for state offices who would let the people vote on prohibition. Back's
resolution passed unanimously, "by a rising vote." The suffrage resolution also passed without dissent. Submitted by thirteen of the nineteen
women in the state Grange and favorably recommended by the all-male
committee on Education and Needed Legislation, it began by protesting
that the world had never "seen a single vested endowment to secure to
woman's calling" the educational advantages provided to men's. Then
it honored the Grange for according women equal rights "within the
gates." That had given women opportunities to show themselves "capable and trustworthy," certainly deserving of the ballot. The suffrage
resolution said nothing about prohibition, but the body considered the
two reforms in quick succession and must surely have seen a connection

between them.[36] Four years later, the Iowa State Grange endorsed equal suffrage with as little apparent controversy. Its historian, agreeing with Douglas Hebb's study of the California State Grange, suggests that the action was intended to win new support for the Order. Membership had fallen precipitously over the previous decade. In their expansive early years, the Iowa historian reports, Grangers showed little interest in the sisters and their causes. But they appealed to women more insistently after membership fell.[37]

Other units supported votes for women less readily. In 1882, for example, a woman member of the Michigan State Grange introduced a resolution demanding "equal rights for women as citizens." It failed to pass. Within the next few years, however, Michigan Grangers edged toward suffrage advocacy. In 1886, a male officer denied that he was a "woman suffragist" but conceded that the alcohol problem was so bad that women should be allowed to vote on prohibition. By the early 1890s, Michigan Grangers consistently supported equal suffrage and happily claimed that their enlightenment had attracted women members.[38] Moving at least as slowly and with somewhat greater commotion, the Delaware State Grange tabled an equal suffrage resolution offered by a subordinate Grange in 1882 and then waited twelve years before returning to the issue. The four women assigned to consider an equal suffrage resolution in 1894 protested that it had been given to them, rather than to a regular committee, "in order to turn it into a farce." Sure that their report would be ridiculed, they proposed that both sexes be required to meet the same educational qualifications and that voting be compulsory for all eligible persons. That won little support. Finally, in 1896, the Delaware State Grange passed an equal suffrage resolution by sixteen votes to nine. One man voted for the resolution while his wife opposed it.[39]

Other state Granges fell into line with more and less alacrity. By 1893, Eliza Gifford, New York's leading equal suffragist, was sure that nearly all of the state bodies had "recognized this principle of equality."[40] Maine called for the "ultimate enfranchisement" of women a year later; New Hampshire, still more cautious, rejected an equal suffrage resolution in 1892 and said nothing in support of the reform until 1902 when Naham Bachelder, its very conservative Master, allowed that New Hampshire Grangers would not oppose equal suffrage if women really wanted it. There was no question of positive support from the New Hampshire State Grange, but most state Granges offered their support, and the National Grange acted, too.[41]

The national body lagged behind some of the states even though it began to consider the question very early, in 1876. Sister Washburn, Lady Assistant Steward of the Colorado State Grange and wife of its Master, introduced an equal suffrage resolution that year and then

chaired the special committee of three men and three women that studied her proposal. The committee recommended its rejection, leaving
Washburn to bring in a minority report. Reminding Grangers that their
Declaration of Purposes pledged them to oppose monopolies, she asked
if "any of my brothers know of a more extensive monopoly than the
monopoly of the elective franchise by the men of this country." The
period's widespread corruption, she added, resulted from "exclusive
man-power." She also argued that women were taxed without representation, that many of them were ignorant of government and needed
the "ballot as an educator," and that the Grange principle of equality
implied support for equal suffrage. Her motion to have the minority
report adopted failed by nine votes to twenty-four. Women members
voted eight to four against it.[42]

The issue arose again in the National Grange of 1885. One of a long
series of resolutions adopted that year announced that the Grange would
"hail with delight any advancement in the legal status of woman, which
may give to her the full right of the ballot-box, and an equal condition of
citizenship." The resolution called that an implication of the Grange position on equality. Its comfortable passage, with twenty-eight votes in favor and eighteen against, suggested that the Grange had taken a firm
stand.[43] Then its gingerly response to an 1886 greeting from the Nebraska
Woman Suffrage Association further defined its position. Mary A. Rhone
of Pennsylvania, who chaired the committee that wrote the Order's reply
to the Nebraska women, held that the suffrage issue should be addressed
in each state Grange, because voting qualifications were a state, not a national, issue. The National Grange acted on that view, and angered some
of the sisters, by striking a clause favoring equal suffrage from the report
of its committee on agriculture.[44] San Jose California sisters expressed
"sorrow and indignation" because blacks could vote and women could
not, and the National Grange did nothing to right the wrong.[45]

Eliza Gifford brought the issue back to the National Grange in 1891.
Then, and again in 1892, it referred her resolutions to the states. Finally,
in 1893, it approved a resolution proposed by its committee on education
that favored "granting to women the same privileges at the ballot-box as
are granted to men."[46] Grange suffragists took that to be the successful
conclusion of their long campaign for the Order's support. But nothing
had been said about the means by which women should be enfranchised;
the Order still had room to waver about state action as opposed to a national constitutional amendment. Grangers had said enough, however, for
suffragists to count them as allies. Susan B. Anthony praised them before
the National American Woman Suffrage Association in 1899, and Gifford
later claimed that the Grange was the "world's greatest equality club."[47]

Grange equal suffrage advocates were understandably optimistic in
the 1890s. Not only had the National Grange endorsed their cause, but

several states had begun to put it into effect. The *Farmer's Friend and Grange Advocate*, organ of the Pennsylvania State Grange, published a chronology of state actions, which included enfranchisement of women for school and municipal purposes in some states and fully equal suffrage in a few others.[48] News from Wyoming and Colorado was especially encouraging. A New Jersey woman told her Pomona Grange in 1893 that the Wyoming legislature had unanimously resolved that equal suffrage reduced crime, poverty, and vice without any harmful side effects, and she was sure that other states could profit as much from the change.[49] Then the *Farmer's Friend* reported that Estelle Reel, formerly of Ohio, had been elected Superintendent of Public Instruction with more votes than any other Republican candidate for Wyoming state office had won. Attractive, young, and single, she carried the cowboy vote by sending out notes on "the daintiest stationary" along with her picture.[50] Still better, the *Farmer's Friend* reprinted an item from the *Woman's Journal*, which reported that 80 percent of the "American women" and few Mexicans were voting in Colorado. Equal suffragists thought that the Colorado returns had buried the canard that only bad women wanted to vote.[51]

But even in the face of such glad news, Grangers still differed about equal suffrage and what they were prepared to do for it. In 1894, for example, a young woman told the Cumberland County, Pennsylvania, Grange that there was much to be said for the reform but that a case could also be made on the other side. She claimed to observe that suffrage advocates were mostly older women who paid too little attention to younger women's interests. If equal suffrage eliminated male chivalry, which "gives as much, if not more, than justice," young women would be net losers. Women would also lose, she thought, because they already had more than enough responsibility for their homes and private philanthropies; voting, which would be morally obligatory for good women if they were to counter the bad, would make their burdens excessive.[52] And John A. McSparran, who became Master of the Pennsylvania State Grange in 1914, ignited a debate in 1909 when he told the *Pennsylvania Grange News* why he had refused to sign a suffrage petition that was pressed upon him at a Grange picnic. He saw no reason to think that women would be better voters than men and, therefore, concluded that letting them vote would simply increase the number of voters and the cost of elections without producing any real improvement. He was also convinced that women were much less interested in public questions than were men. Girls, he observed, participated less than boys in school debates, and women in the state Grange rarely led debates even on temperance, which was supposed to be their special interest.[53] McSparran's extraordinary argument started a lively debate in the *News*, which seemed to be resolved when the Pennsylvania State Grange unanimously passed a suffrage resolution in 1910.[54] But some opposition continued. In 1914, for example, the Pennsylvania State Grange Pomona used part of her annual report to say that "women should be content to stay at home and look after the comfort of family instead of demanding the ballot," and the session took time to hear an "anti-suffragette of New Jersey." It also heard a speech favoring equal suffrage by a Boston woman, along with supporting comments from Leonard Rhone, who had been Master of the state Grange for eighteen years, and by its woman's work committee.[55] Equal suffrage had some remaining opponents, but they were badly overshadowed in that meeting.

The woman who raised the suffrage issue in the 1910 Pennsylvania State Grange asked for more than passage of a resolution. She also wanted members to circulate petitions calling for a suffrage amendment to the national constitution, which an encouraging number of them did.[56] Her request left action to individuals, rather than putting the Grange to work for equal suffrage in some institutional way. The Order customarily left suffrage work to individuals. Hoping for greater exertions by the organization itself, Jennie Buell complained in 1912 that the Grange had "never . . . campaigned for its belief"; it had never backed its resolutions with a really concerted effort. Then the Michigan State Grange took extraordinary measures.[57]

Michigan's legislature submitted a state constitutional amendment enfranchising women to the voters in 1912. By that time, women were voting in several western states, and Agnes Riddle, secretary of the Colorado State Grange, was a legislator. But no state east of the Mississippi had yet followed the west's example. The Michigan State Grange favored the amendment, but a brother told its executive committee that the Grange position was far too little known. He had talked to a legislator who was unaware of it. Then the executive committee instructed the legislative committee to concentrate on the suffrage issue in cooperation with the woman's work committee, the state Grange Lecturer, who was then Jennie Buell, and Ida Chittenden, an active suffragist and Granger who raised violets in Lansing. Like Buell, Chittenden was a self-supporting, single, normal school graduate who combined Grange work with a wide range of other civic activities. Buell and Chittenden opened a Grange suffrage office in Lansing from which they tried to inspire Grangers throughout the state to support the suffrage amendment. They distributed suffrage songs to local Granges and brought the state Grange together with other rural groups, the Gleaners and Farmers' Clubs, to issue a joint statement for equal suffrage. It said that suffrage opponents were a coalition of "brewery associations, patent medicine corporations, white slave dealers, etc.," while the moral elements of society supported the amendment. Good people knew that women voters would improve the electorate; only 2 percent of Michigan's criminals, women were more likely than men to graduate from high school and strongly supported "sanitation, pure food, the proper control of penal institutions and asylums, social purity, child labor, and the control of that worst of evils— the white slave traffic.[58] The amendment passed in rural areas but was not adopted because the votes of two counties were disqualified. Though bitterly disappointed, Buell persevered in the cause until Michigan passed a suffrage amendment six years later.

As suffrage passed in a growing list of states, then nationally, no Grange repeated the public campaign that Buell and Chittenden had made on behalf of the Michigan body in 1912. But many Grangers kept the issue before the Order itself. They used all of the familiar arguments, but also changed their thinking in two ways. First, the National Grange decided that equal suffrage should be obtained by amending the national constitution rather than by action in every state. C. B. Kegley, Master of the Washington State Grange and an outspoken Grange progressive, asked for support of a national constitutional amendment in 1914; his proposal failed after a long discussion, but the Grange passed a resolution favoring equal suffrage in principle. It voted in favor of a national amendment in 1915, although opposition was strong enough to force the only roll call in that year's meeting. Thirty members favored a national amendment in 1915; twenty-five still thought that the issue should be fought out in each state. The barely successful resolution came to the floor with the support of a new standing committee on woman's suffrage, which C. B. Kegley chaired. Its report summarized two generations of argument. The Grange was committed to equality; where women voted, they fostered refinement, sobriety, and families; and women should vote because they are fully equal to men.[59]

The Grange supported a national amendment, without requiring a roll call, in 1916. It repeated that in 1917, when the committee on woman's suffrage argued that the adoption of equal suffrage in New York showed that "final victory" was close. Women would vote despite the "united opposition of the liquor forces of the land, and . . . the foolish White House picketing and other extreme and unnecessary measures of its friends."[60]

World War I brought another change in the case for equal suffrage. Many Grangers noted, as did their suffrage committee, that the war was requiring women to assume new responsibilities. In 1918, for example, the *National Grange Monthly* reported that women were taking increased responsibility in the Order. It ran a picture of a young Missouri woman who served as Master of her local Grange and an admiring story about a fifteen-year-old girl who was Lecturer of a Grange in New Hampshire. The Lecturer not only helped to keep the Grange going during the war but also did "extensive knitting and other Red Cross work."[61] A more adventurous woman, a teacher and former Lecturer of a Massachusetts

Grange, told the *National Grange Monthly* in 1918 that she had spent that summer doing "strenuous work on the soil" as a "farmerette." She had lived in a house provided by a "philanthropically inclined lady of Boston" with other young women who were mostly students and graduates of Smith, Vassar, Boston University, and other colleges. They "wore uniforms consisting of khaki bloomers and middy blouses" when they went out to help neighboring farmers. The farmers had been doubtful at first, she recalled, but had come to appreciate their help. She urged Grangers to encourage the farmerettes because educated young women who had satisfying experiences on the land would bring favorable impressions of farmers and farming back to their usual circles.[62]

The Order's interest in farmerettes probably extended little beyond that one woman and her article. But Grangers found many occasions to say that women were proving themselves in new ways during the war. A New Jersey woman made that point in a talk to her Pomona Grange by quoting an Englishman who said that women's war efforts proved that they could do "anything with practice." She added that war experiences had ended "the delusion of ages, that woman's work must consist only in the performance of household duties." Discounting old claims to distinctiveness further, she doubted that "any great reform will come at once with the inauguration of woman suffrage." Women's votes would not dramatically elevate public life. Their enfranchisement would only be "one step" in the progress of democracy, but it would alleviate "sex antagonism" by ending an injustice that had long embittered women.[63]

The argument for equal suffrage, and about women's rights more generally, might have taken new directions in the Grange after that. Some familiar ideas were being challenged. But, instead, the debate stopped because Grangers, like most other suffrage advocates, thought that the nineteenth amendment had settled the question. They later offered occasional suggestions about ways of encouraging women to use the franchise but were generally content to close the file on equal suffrage. After more than forty years of debate, most of them had come to accept a standard justification for the reform. It was a matter of right, a clear implication of the Order's enlightened tradition, and a prerequisite for other reforms. Emphases varied, but the standard argument was straightforward and familiar. Seeing no need to consider it further, Grange women turned increasingly to home economics, a rubric that covered a wide range of domestic and civic aspirations. It would be the great focus of Grange women's activity for the next half-century.

NOTES

1. Nordin, *Rich Harvest*, 193; Woods, *Knights of the Plow*, 168–170 recognizes that the "early Grange was not a leader in promoting women's suffrage" and

then argues that male Grangers defined women's role in the Order and in society in terms of what he takes to have been their republican ideology. Borrowing from Linda K. Kerber, *Women of the Republic: Intellect and Ideology in Revolutionary America* (Chapel Hill: University of North Carolina Press, 1980), Woods suggests that Grangers saw women as "Republican Mothers" who trained their sons to be republican citizens and reinforced their husbands' virtue.

2. Hebb, "The Woman Movement in the California State Grange", 62; Smith, *The History of the Iowa State Grange*, 5–6.

3. Studies of the equal suffrage campaign that provide background information for this chapter include: Eleanor Flexner, *Century of Struggle: The Woman's Rights Movement in the United States* (New York: Atheneum, 1971), especially Chapters 10 and 13; Linda K. Kerber and Jane DeHart-Mathews, *Women's America: Refocusing the Past* (New York: Oxford University Press, 1987), which reprints two chapters from Anne F. Scott and Andrew M. Scott, *One Half the People: The Fight for Woman Suffrage* (Philadelphia: J. B. Lippincott, 1975); Paula Baker, "The Domestication of Politics: Women and American Political Society, 1780–1920," *The American Historical Review* 89 (June 1984): 620–47, which is a guide to suffrage historiography, very little of which bears specifically on rural women's participation in the movement; Hebb, "The Woman Movement in the California State Grange," deals specifically with Grange women's participation; Steven M. Buechler, *The Transformation of the Woman Suffrage Movement: The Case of Illinois, 1850–1920* (New Brunswick: Rutgers University Press, 1986), 49–52 offers a periodization of the suffrage movement that is very generally suggestive for understanding Grange women's participation; Aileen Kraditor, *The Ideas of the Woman Suffrage Movement, 1890–1920* (New York: W. W. Norton, 1981), Chapter 3, offers categories that have shaped much of the historical discussion of suffrage arguments, including this chapter. Kraditor demonstrates that suffragists began by arguing that women had a natural right to civil equality and then shifted to an argument from "expediency," which claimed that women's votes were needed to win prohibition and other reforms. Grange women clearly stressed the argument from expediency, though some of them continued the earlier natural rights argument, too.

4. D. Wyatt Aiken, *The Patrons of Husbandry*, Bryan Fund Publication No. 6, National Grange, n.d. (originally published in the June 1872 *Rural Carolinian*); Aiken, *The Grange*, 14.

5. William E. Simmon, *How I Came to be a Patron*, Bryan Fund Publication No. 2, National Grange, n.d. (originally published in the December 1871 *Rural Carolinian*).

6. Capt. E. L. Hovey, *Speech to Farmer's Festival at St. Johnsbury, Vermont, February 22, 1872*, a Bryan Fund Publication, National Grange, n.d.; Guy B. Horton, *A History of the Grange in Vermont* (Montpelier: Vermont State Grange, 1926), 52; Woods, *Knights of the Plow*, 169 cites Hovey on the importance of women's domestic responsibility. Hovey, according to Woods, "encapsulated" the Grange doctrine of "Republican Motherhood."

7. A. B. Smedley, *Principles and Aims of the Patrons of Husbandry* (Burlington, Iowa: R. T. Root, 1874), 33.

8. *Pacific Rural Press* 7 (28 March 1874): 196.

9. Reuben Brigham, "Grange Progress in Maryland," manuscript dated 11

December 1922 in Archives of the Maryland State Grange, Historical Manuscripts and Archives Department, University of Maryland College Park Libraries.

10. *Journal of Proceedings of the Third Annual Session of the Ohio State Grange*, 1876, 53–56.

11. *Bulletin* 3 (July 1877).

12. Gardner, *The Grange*, 517–19.

13. Grosh, *Mentor in the Granges and Homes of Patrons of Husbandry*, 119–24.

14. *Indiana Farmer* 9 (7 February 1874): 3.

15. *Dirigo Rural* 1 (26 December 1874): 194; 3 (22 April 1876): 3.

16. *Proceedings of the New Hampshire State Grange* (1876):4.

17. *Proceedings of the Wisconsin State Grange* (1875):84; Elizabeth Cady Stanton, Susan B. Anthony, and Matilda Joslyn Gage, *History of Woman Suffrage* (New York: Arno Press, 1969), 3: 288, 515, 530.

18. Hebb, "The Woman Movement in the California State Grange," 44–45, 48, 52–53, 121.

19. *The Husbandman* 1 (20 January 1875): 1.

20. Ibid. (17 February 1875): 5.

21. Ibid. (2 October 1875): 5.

22. Ibid. (10 November 1875): 2; 18 (24 February 1892): 2.

23. Ibid. 1 (10 November 1875): 2.

24. Ibid. (22 December 1875): 5; (2 February 1876): 4–5.

25. Ibid. (1 March 1876): 2.

26. Ibid. 3 (21 February 1877): 2.

27. *Grange Visitor* 9 (15 December 1883): 2.

28. *Hennepin County Mirror* 11 (3 February 1882): 5; 12 (6 October 1882): 1.

29. *The Husbandman* 17 (8 October 1890): 2.

30. Nordin, *Rich Harvest*, 191.

31. *Journal of Proceedings of the Tenth Annual Session of the Rhode Island State Grange*, 1896, 8–9.

32. *Journal of Proceedings of the Sixth Annual Session of the Rhode Island State Grange*, 1893, 26.

33. Eliza Gifford, address to the New York State Grange, February 1894, in Gifford manuscripts, Patterson Library and Art Gallery.

34. Ibid.; *Farmer's Friend and Grange Advocate* 21 (6 October 1894): 1.

35. *Farmer's Friend and Grange Advocate* 21 (6 October 1894): 1.

36. *Proceedings of the Eleventh Annual Session of the Indiana State Grange, Patrons of Husbandry*, 1881, 28–30.

37. Smith, *The History of the Iowa State Grange*, 5–6.

38. Trump, *The Grange in Michigan*, 29, 36, 48, 50.

39. Passmore, *History of the Delaware State Grange*, 26, 60, 63.

40. *Farmer's Friend and Grange Advocate* 21 (6 October 1894): 1.

41. Sherman, "The Grange in Maine and New Hampshire," 224.

42. *Journal of Proceedings of the Tenth Annual Session of the National Grange*, 1876, 94, 121, 169–71; *Colorado State Grange History* (Denver: State Grange, 1975), 15–16, 22.

43. *Journal of Proceedings of the Nineteenth Annual Session of the National Grange*, 1885, 105–7.

44. *Journal of Proceedings of the Twentieth Annual Session of the National Grange*, 1886, 139, 144–45.

45. *Grange Visitor* 12 (15 April 1887): 5.

46. *Journal of Proceedings of the Twenty-Fifth Annual Session of the National Grange*, 1891, 39, 130; *Twenty-Sixth Annual Session*, 1892, 168–69; *Twenty-Seventh Annual Session*, 1893, 89.

47. *National Grange Monthly* 14 (December 1917): 15–16; Eliza C. Gifford, address to the New York State Grange, February 1914, in Gifford manuscripts, Patterson Library and Art Gallery; Anthony and Harper, eds., *History of Woman Suffrage*, 4:327.

48. *Farmer's Friend and Grange Advocate* 23 (12 December 1896): 1.

49. Ibid. 20 (16 September 1893): 1.

50. Ibid. 22 (12 January 1895): 1.

51. Ibid. 21 (16 June 1894): 1.

52. Ibid. 21 (9 June 1894): 1.

53. *Pennsylvania Grange News* 6 (November 1909): 111.

54. Ibid. 6 (January 1910): 35.

55. Ibid. 11 (January 1915): 129.

56. Ibid.

57. *National Grange Monthly* 9 (July 1912): 5.

58. Ibid. (August 1912): 13; (April 1913): 7; Leonard, *Woman's Who's Who of America*, 76.

59. *Journal of Proceedings of the Forty-Eighth Annual Session of the National Grange*, 1914, 149; *Forty-Ninth Annual Session*, 1915, 9, 142–3; Gardner, *The Grange*, 198–200.

60. *Journal of Proceedings of the National Grange of the Patrons of Husbandry Fifty-First Annual Session*, 1917, 191.

61. *National Grange Monthly* 15 (July 1918): 6, 15.

62. Ibid. 15 (September 1918): 17; Whitehead, *Women in American Farming*, has several references to farmerettes and the Women's Land Army.

63. *National Grange Monthly* 14 (December 1917): 15; 15 (March 1918): 8.

7

Remaining Tasks and Recent Changes

Grange women reached some deeply satisfying milestones in the years around 1920. The nineteenth amendment secured the votes that some of them had pursued for half a century; the eighteenth amendment imposed prohibition; and home economics departments were proliferating in agricultural colleges. Long struggles concluded, and some women felt that an era of reform had ended with them. "Prohibitionists and Equal Suffragists fell silent," Charlotte Perkins Gilman observed.[1] But Dora H. Stockman, a leading Granger from the 1910s through the 1940s, denied that success had brought the women of her Order to the end of their progressive history. Liquor had been driven underground for a time thanks partly to Grange women, but the battle against cigarettes had just begun. Women could vote, but the Grange example of equality between the genders had not yet influenced cooperative marketing organizations, in which women took little part. Grange women still had plenty to do, Stockman insisted, even after winning some of their most protracted battles.[2]

An influential historian makes a broadly similar point. The year 1920 really is an "obvious benchmark in the history of women in politics in the United States," Nancy Cott recognizes, but too much emphasis on the suffrage amendment, she cautions, can obscure some important continuities, notably the fact that women characteristically pursued public ends through private, voluntary associations after 1920, just as they had through most of the nineteenth century. Cott cites a 1933 study, which suggests that women may actually have been "*over*organized" then, and she calls its appended list of women's organizations "staggering." Clearly, reform-minded women did not believe that their tradition of voluntary action had been superceded by electoral politics in 1920; that century-old tradition continued in many forms.[3] Dora Stockman, leader of the third generation of Michigan Grange women, following Mary Mayo and Jennie Buell, helped to sustain it in the Grange. She also exemplifies some marked continuities in the character of Grange leadership.

Stockman's life closely paralleled her predecessors'. "I come of early pioneer American stock," her autobiographical essay proudly begins. Her parents moved from New York to Michigan in 1869, took up a homestead, and joined the Grange in 1874, two years after Dora Stockman was born in their log cabin. She passed a teaching examination at the age of fourteen, began teaching at age sixteen, and married one year later. She and her husband farmed unsuccessfully for two years and then opened a store in Arcadia, a village on the shore of Lake Michigan, near the northern end of the lower peninsula. Soon a "saloon and two blind pigs, together with a German beer garden," persuaded the couple to move a few miles farther north, to Benzonia. By that time, she had taken a correspondence course on domestic science and another, surely on some aspect of religion, from the Moody Bible Institute. Then she "finished the required work for a literary course" at the Congregational College in Benzonia. She also wrote a thesis on "The Present Day Influence of the Life of Christ"; The American Sunday School Mission published it as *A Bountiful Harvest*. After a brief sojourn on the west coast, intended to relieve her husband's bronchial complaints, the Stockmans returned to Michigan. He started a new farm while she studied at Hillsdale College, where she won election to the Ladies' Literary Union, which was a mark of real distinction, and earned an A.B. degree in 1903. Then she joined her husband on the farm, taught school to supplement the family income, bore two children, contributed to Grange publications, and wrote two children's books. In 1930, after sixteen years as Lecturer of the Michigan State Grange, Stockman began work toward a doctorate in sociology at Michigan State College; she never finished her dissertation, but in 1934, she became the first woman to receive an honorary Doctor of Laws degree from Michigan State. A member of the Michigan House of Representatives from 1938 to 1946, she supported state aid to schools, school lunch programs, a plan for additional years of high school that foreshadowed community colleges, and heavy taxes on alcohol and tobacco. Widowed in 1932, she married again in 1946 and died two years later.[4]

Stockman broadly resembled earlier women Grange leaders. Nearly all of them had been old stock Americans, sometime teachers, more than commonly educated, and devoted to Protestant religion. And like many of her predecessors, Stockman had literary ambition and used her writing to promote ideas that they would have heartily approved. She was especially proud of *Farmerkin's Farm Rhymes*, a slim book of children's verse from which Silver Burdette, a well-known schoolbook publisher, chose eight poems for its anthologies. The verses evoked the "wonders" of rural childhood in order to inspire love of nature and "keep young people on the farm." "My Pansy Bed" is a typical example.

> I planted purple pansy seeds
>   in my little garden spaces,
> And when I went a-picking them
>   Found rows of baby-faces.

The rest of the collection presents equally simple images of flowers, animals, and other bucolic delights. Stockman had less than delightful experiences on farms; she remembered her parents' "almost worthless soil" and the failure of the first farm that she operated with her husband. Preferring town to farm life, the Stockmans "put a man on the farm" and moved to Lansing in 1914 when she began her long service as Lecturer of the state Grange. However, *Farmerkin's Farm Rhymes* gives no hint of that.[5]

She intended her *Book of Dialogs* for young people who were "too timid or obstinate to give a recitation or declamation" but might take part in a skit or play. Jennie Buell told Lecturers that they were responsible for making silent Grangers speak; Stockman, a long-time Lecturer, wrote the *Dialogs* to help silent children find their voices. The *Dialogs* also teach patriotism, which was the point of her "Flag Exercise for Memorial Day," and moral virtues. "Neenah's Gratitude," a skit intended for Columbus Day, combines the two. It concerns two white children who had been raised by Indians but instinctively feel that their light skin and curly hair make them superior to their associates. They are returned to their natural parents by a noble Indian woman who remembered the kindnesses that whites had done for her. Another little play, "The Shadow On The Home," describes a man who torments his family by spending what little money he earns at "Tom O'Brien's saloon."[6]

Sometime between 1914 and 1920 Stockman also wrote, but did not publish, a novel entitled *Happy Valley*. It concerns two young men who study agriculture and engineering at an institution that sounds very much like Michigan State. They go north to fight a forest fire, earn a sizable reward from a lumber company, acquire land on which they mean to develop a farm and a sawmill, nearly lose their title to a repulsive trickster, and finally win a richly deserved success. One of them courts an immensely worthy young woman who is at first ashamed of her rustic upbringing but learns that she has "the things that really give a woman true culture." Towns are full of "sham," Stockman teaches, but

"Nature is sincere and honest; she knows no deceit." The naturally virtuous young woman, the novel's other sterling characters, its descriptions of an idyllic place, and the role of a friendly capitalist who intends benign development of "Happy Valley" are all reminiscent of Gene Stratton-Porter's slightly earlier novels.[7] Stockman's celebration of rustic virtue, particularly the young woman's, also continues a long tradition of Grange moralizing.

Stockman had an exceptional knowledge of Grange traditions. Not only did she grow up in the Order and give it many years of service, but she wrote much of a doctoral dissertation about it as well. Surviving chapters concern Michigan Grange history, "What Granges Actually Do," and "Women in the Grange." The last chapter honors Mary Mayo, especially for her work on behalf of women at the Michigan Agriculture College, and acknowledges Stockman's own place in Michigan's succession of women leaders. She was proud that every Michigan State Grange Lecturer for thirty-six years had been a woman and that women nearly monopolized Lecturers' posts in the state's subordinate and Pomona Granges as well. As Lecturers and through their special committees, Stockman plausibly argued, women directed the Order's educational work. She thought that prepared them for service to public education; Stockman herself won two twelve-year terms, starting in 1919, on the state Board of Agriculture, which was the governing authority of the Michigan Agricultural College. She was the first woman to hold elective office in Michigan.[8]

Stockman's emphasis on women Lecturers certainly reflected her own experience, but it was also an apt generalization about her sisters. Women were probably the majority of local Grange Lecturers at the beginning of this century. Moreover, the number serving in her own post, as state Grange Lecturers, rose late in Stockman's career and continued upward until the 1970s, when women nearly monopolized the office. In 1930, twelve out of thirty-six state Grange Lecturers were women. Their number increased to nineteen out of thirty-six in 1935, twenty-three out of thirty-eight in 1940, twenty-eight out of thirty-seven in 1955, and thirty-five out of thirty-eight in 1975. Women's share of other state offices increased very little through the same period. In 1975, for example, only two relatively small state Granges, in South Dakota and North Carolina, had women Masters, two states had women Treasurers, and twenty-three had women Secretaries. Lecturing, as Stockman understood very accurately, was and would long remain women's most important and characteristic leadership role in the Grange.[9]

Stockman was equally right and prescient about the importance of women's committees. Grange women have long controlled their own specialized committees or departments. They have served on others, particularly committees interested in education and health, since the

Order's first decade but have channeled most of their energy into juvenile and home economics work. Until very recently, women managed juvenile Grange work almost alone; a long succession of National Grange Juvenile Superintendents, an office created in 1922, were women. That continued the Grange tradition, which goes back at least to the woman's work committees in the 1880s and 1890s, of making women responsible for getting children interested in the Order. And women have entirely controlled home economics work since 1919, when men stopped serving on the National Grange home economics committee. At about the same time, the committee broadened its focus beyond scientific housekeeping to include everything that interested women and everything that Grange leaders thought that women ought to do for the Order. The 1926 national committee report indicated the subject's breadth by urging state home economics committees to consider food, clothing, child care, home sanitation, and the Order's social and educational functions. It asked local committees to augment their Lecturers' efforts by conducting supplemental classes on literature, music, and other edifying topics.[10] Home economics committees, as the principal channel for women's participation in the Grange, were natural allies of Lecturers, who were the principal women officers.

Through most of the 1920s, reports of the national home economics committee suggested topics for discussion and a variety of general and specific goals but described few concrete actions of its own or of its state and local counterparts. The reports mainly exhorted state and local committees, and Grange women generally, to be diligent and versatile in doing good. In 1926 and 1927, they urged state and local Granges to form committees; many had not done so. And they asked the committees to see that every Grange got a picture of Caroline Hall to hang in its gallery of founders, protest advertisements that showed women smoking, urge members to keep their excessively mobile families home for recreation at least once a week, and try to improve the outward appearance of their Grange halls. In 1928, the committee again urged women to improve the looks of their Grange halls and of nearby school grounds. It also asked home economics committees to encourage family reading; its suggested reading list included Kipling's *Puck of Pook's Hill*, *Rewards and Fairies*, and *The Jungle Book*, among other mostly English titles. Finally, it exhorted state and local committees to protest smoking by women and girls, marathon dances, alcohol, and narcotics. It wanted Granges to press their neighborhood schools to indoctrinate children against the last two evils.[11]

Soon after the national committee made its hortatory 1828 report, the *National Grange Monthly* offered a concrete example of what local home economics committees could do. The women of Plattekill Grange in Ulster County, New York, had raised $489.39 by conducting dances, suppers, and other activities that provided "a continuously helpful social time" for the Grange and the community at large. They used the money to reduce the debt on their Grange hall and buy an oil stove, pitchers, glasses, waste baskets, artificial fruit for Pomona's desk, candles and candlesticks, and a briefcase for the Secretary. They also cleaned the hall, groomed the grounds, planted flowers, solicited a donation of gravel and got the brothers to fill a muddy hole in front of the hall, celebrated National Bird Week by conducting an essay contest for local school children, arranged exhibits by those same children at their Grange fair, mounted a display of their own produce at the Ulster County Fair, got their entire Grange to worship together on "Go-to-Church Sunday," circulated a protest petition when a reduction in local mail service was threatened, took up a Thanksgiving collection for a widowed mother of six, conducted Grange programs for Better Homes Week and Mother's Day, and contributed to the state Grange scholarship fund. That was an impressive, and surely exceptional, amount of work for an eight-member committee.[12]

The 1929 report also scattered suggestions about moral reform and intellectual cultivation but focused on an alarming theme suggested by Theodore Roosevelt. Worried about the state of American country life, Roosevelt had preached that American civilization depended on "the wholesomeness, the attractiveness, and the completeness, as well as the prosperity of life in the country." And Alfred Vivian, an active Granger and Dean of the College of Agriculture at Ohio State, observed that too many farm households were unattractive to their young, who got less attention than cattle and hogs. The result was that young people fled the land and America's essential rural communities were losing their futures. Grangers, the committee suggested, could forestall national ruin by making their homes attractive to children and instructive to neighbors.

The 1929 report also included brief descriptions of what home economics committees were doing in some of the best-organized states. In Massachusetts, subordinate Grange committees had contributed to the restoration of a farm house, which served as the Home Economics Practice House on the state college campus at Amherst. A *Boston Globe* account said that 150 Granges had contributed. The college had solicited their help through Hadley Grange woman who belonged to the Woman's Advisory Committee on the Practice House.[13] Similarly, Pennsylvania's state committee had earned $10,000 for a women's dormitory at the Pennsylvania State College by publishing a cookbook that sold 30,000 copies. The state Grange had promised to raise money for a dormitory in 1922; when the committee responsible for fund raising stipulated that it be a women's dormitory, the home economics committee offered to help. The fact that Clara Phillips, a prominent Washington County

Granger and a member of the state committee, had become the college's first woman trustee in 1926 must surely have strengthened the committee's interest.[14] Also devoted to education, New York's committee had raised money for a scholarship fund and had sponsored speaking contests in public schools and a "Little Play contest at county fairs." At the same time, Michigan's committee was working to see that school children got hot lunches, every rural school had a first aid kit, and farm women made use of the Michigan State College extension service.[15]

The home economics work described in 1929's state reports consisted mostly of services to education, but later activities were more characteristically diverse. In 1930, for example, the Rhode Island State Grange home economics committee worked with other organizations to restrict billboards. It tried to persuade farmers not to provide land for the eyesores and companies to advertise only in commercial areas. It also offered silver loving cups for especially fine home and Grange hall beautification projects. The Pennsylvania State Grange committee offered five-dollar prizes to Granges which reported that all of their women members had voted; that was a rare echo of the suffrage crusades. A prominent sister had reported two years earlier that only 40,000 out of a possible 400,000 Pennsylvania women had voted in a recent presidential election.[16] At the subordinate level, the home economics committee of the Coldwater, Michigan, Grange held a Halloween party in order to reduce vandalism in the area; the National Grange committee advised suburban Granges to hold similar parties. And an Oregon Grange lightened its members' work by operating a laundry. Farms in its neighborhood had yet to receive electricity, so the Grange home economics committee rented a room in a village that had power, got hot water and steam from the creamery next door, bought an electric washer, and scheduled members for two-hour sessions. The facility was popular, even though women had to haul their wash to town.

The range of projects described in the 1930 report reflected Grange women's diverse circumstances. The Oregon sisters needed to lighten their work; the old problem of drudgery, which had dropped out of the national committee's pronouncemenst, was still with them. Women in Coldwater, Michigan, were more concerned about vandalism, and the sisters in Rhode Island wanted to preserve some of their densely populated state's rural beauty. Grange women were more and less preoccupied with their personal needs, more and less free to consider matters of public welfare. The national committee made that point a little differently by observing that home economics work could be rewarding for women who had immediate, personal concerns about their homes and children and also for women whose children had grown up and who wanted a socially beneficial use for their increased leisure. The preponderance of community service projects over enterprises like the

Oregon laundry suggests that relatively fortunate and disinterested women were most involved in home economics work.[17]

The national committee's abstracts of state and local reports suggest that really successful home economics activities were much less than universal. In 1931, the national committee reported that thirteen of the thirty-two state Granges had begun the year without standing home economics committees. They had session committees that met during state Grange meetings to write reports that were "merely essays on the value of homes, or some kindred subjects." Such essays had been standard elements in Grange programs almost from the Order's beginning; most of the reports issued by the old woman's work committees and by the national home economics committee itself had been effusions on "homes, or some kindred subjects." But the woman who chaired the national committee from 1931 to 1934 was impatient with rhetoric.

Ethel J. Hammond came to the committee with an extraordinary range of experience. Educated at the Laconia, New Hampshire, High School, she had gone on to Plymouth Normal School, received some additional instruction at Harvard and Oxford, and taught psychology at Plymouth Normal School before she married. Hammond was an active member of the Laconia Congregational Church, President of the Laconia Woman's Club, Master of her subordinate Grange, and a member of the New Hampshire legislature. Elected in 1930, with both Republican and Democratic nominations, she considered herself an independent Republican. Hammond complained that newspapers ignored the sixteen women who served with 400 male legislators, but allowed that the men, though they generated irritating clouds of tobacco smoke, treated the minority fairly. Hammond had little impact on either the clouds or legislation.[18]

She wanted to get more substantial results from Grange home economics committees, so she wrote to the state Grange Masters and got all of them to appoint standing committees that were to function as the second level in a hierarchy. Each member of the national committee was to supervise a set of state committees; each state committee was to supervise committee work in Pomona Granges; and the Pomona committees were to supervise home economics committees in subordinate and juvenile Granges. The national committee also published a list of specific suggestions for projects of service to the Grange itself. Local home economics committees were to prepare lists of Grangers who were eligible for honors, conduct special meetings on Grange anniversaries, work with juvenile Granges, get people to subscribe to the *National Grange Monthly*, and cooperate with extension workers to disseminate knowledge of home economics.

Despite their clarified structure and charge, home economics committees remained less than universally vigorous. The most active state groups, the national committee reported in 1931, were in Oregon, Pennsylvania, Massachusetts, New Jersey, New Hampshire, New York, and Kansas. With the exceptions of Oregon and Pennsylvania, those states had fewer than the average complement of women among their principal leaders. Perhaps women's efforts were more narrowly channeled in those states than elsewhere.[19] However that may have been, the national committee judged that Kansas "probably has the strongest all round committee in the country." The exemplary group had been created in 1916 and merged in 1920 with the vigorous Kansas woman's work committee, which had revived in 1906. In 1931, it organized a contest in order to encourage home beautification and community service projects. The Kansas women were very specific about the things that made homes beautiful. They wanted members to plant flowers, shrubs, and trees; they wanted chickens, machinery, and clothes lines kept away from front lawns.[20]

A year later, the national committee reported that the Kansans and others whom it had commended in 1931 were still doing good work and that most other states also had active committees. Only four had reported no accomplishments, and they had prospects of improvement. Indiana sisters were working with home economics clubs outside of the Grange, and Michigan's efforts were sure to increase because Dora Stockman had accepted the state committee's chairmanship. Activities in the better organized states were, as usual, diverse. Committees in some of the southern states, where Granges had lately revived after a twenty- to thirty-year hiatus, were encouraging women to garden and can produce. The national committee, indirectly and uncharacteristically acknowledging the depression, commended canning as a way to maintain children's nutrition in "these present emergency times." The New England and Middle Atlantic committees were working to retain members, as the National Grange Master had asked home economics committees to do. And committees in various places were holding home economics conferences during state Grange meetings; a few brothers had attended the program in California. The committees' names reflected the diversity of their work. Five states had Home and Community Welfare Committees, two had Home Community Committees, and New York had a Hospitality and Service Committee. Their titles meant to indicate the breadth of the committees' interests—to show that they were not wholly domestic—but the national committee complained that variety was confusing and hoped that all of the women's committees could soon agree on a common name. The issue was finally resolved in 1967, when the National Grange Home Economics Committee became the Committee on Women's Activities, a name reminiscent of the earlier woman's work committees. It recognized that the newer group's responsibility had expanded to the breadth of its predecessors'.[21]

Home economics work, under its various names, continued along its various lines through the 1930s and 1940s. Committees encouraged church attendance by sponsoring special "Go-to-Church" Sundays, conducted contests in domestic crafts, improved their Grange halls, helped Lecturers with programs, and raised money for charity and in aid of churches. During World War II, they promoted home gardens, canning, and Red Cross projects. They prepared surgical dressings and made scrapbooks with jokes, poems, crossword puzzles, American flags, and other diverting or comforting items for hospitalized soldiers. They bought war bonds, enough in Connecticut to sponsor a Flying Fortress called the "Connecticut Granger," served as air raid wardens and plane spotters, and sent gifts to Grangers in the military. They were as patriotic as home economics committees had been during World War I and probably more industrious about it.[22]

Then the national committee responded to cold war anxieties by asking whether "the homes of Rural America" were doing "everything possible toward our Nation's Security at the present time?" National security, in the committee's view, required a firm stand against "indecent reading material on the book stands, moving pictures which are degrading to adult minds, to say nothing of the effect on youth," juvenile delinquency, and "shady road houses." The committee urged its state and local counterparts to help their Lecturers fight such evils, especially indecent movies and books. It also fostered Blue Cross insurance schemes, assistance to youth groups such as 4-H and the Future Farmers of America, various sewing contests, and aid to rural churches. Church projects were the major emphasis in 1947, when committees raised money to make pastors' studies more comfortable and to augment their salaries, provided transportation for people attending churches and Sunday schools, and observed "Rural Life Sunday" and "Go-to-Church Sunday." The national committee said that neglected rural churches needed all of the help that the Grange could provide.[23]

Women's committees never entirely neglected community service, but contests, particularly in sewing, attracted increasing interest starting about 1950, when the national committee found a helpful sponsor in the Spool Cotton Company; it provided awards for every level of Grange competition. In 1951, the Sears-Roebuck Foundation Educational Bureau increased competitive fervor by providing electric sewing machines to first- and second-prize winners in the national adult and juvenile competitions. The Foundation also sponsored a Grange Quilt Contest, which especially interested older women, who had not participated much in other contests. State winners got fifty dollars and then presented their quilts to the first ladies of their states in exchange for a moment or more of fame. In 1954, for example, fourteen women from the Middletown Valley Grange in Maryland lunched with Gov. and Mrs. Theodore R. McKeldin, who had received their winning quilt late the previous year.

The Maryland Farmer devoted a half page, with a proportionately large picture, to the occasion. It was extraordinary coverage of a women's event, much the largest item about women that a Maryland Grange leader collected for his scrapbook.[24] But the women of Virginville Grange in Pennsylvania, who won the national competition and its $1,000 prize, eclipsed their Maryland competitors by visiting the White House to give their quilt to Mamie Eisenhower. The first lady and her husband spent half an hour with the Grangers, who considered the visit a "never-to-be-forgotten experience."[25] Quilting had come a long way in the scale of Grange values since 1912, when a national home economics committee announced that scientific homemaking had superceded such antique crafts.[26]

Really lucrative competitions, particularly the National Grange $50,000 Sewing Contest, began in the late 1950s. In order to insure widespread participation, the national committee assigned quotas to each state. Kansas, for example, exceeded its goal of 1,330 dresses by producing 1,497 in 1958, the contest's first year.[27] A comparable baking contest began in 1959; prizes included electric stoves and trips to National Bake Offs, which were held during National Grange meetings. Both contests depended on commercial sponsors. In 1966, for example, the Chrysler Company gave a Dodge Dart, the New York Fur Dressers gave a mink stole, and the American Printed Fabrics Council gave a weekend for two in New York City.[28]

Attractive as contests became, Grange women in the 1950s and later continued to find time for service projects and their traditional literary work. In 1960, for example, California women published a collection of their original poetry, *California Golden Inspirations*, to raise money for their service projects. "The Grange," written by a Lake Francis sister, is characteristic of the book.

> Up in the hills where I live
> There's nothing much to see
> What little time to the meetings I give
> I learn things that are good for me."[29]

Such traditional activities continued, but Grange women increasingly emphasized contests. In 1978, when an *Indianapolis Star* reporter asked the new Director of Women's Activities for the Indiana State Grange about the farm protests, which were then exceptionally intense, the Director said that "women's activities consist mostly of contests in sewing, crocheting, needlework and baking." Grange women certainly cared about farm problems, but they left such matters to the brothers.[30] The brothers, in turn, left contests to the sisters. Very few wandered into women's domain; in 1985, a Pennsylvania boy won third place in Class

D, the "Boys and Girls" section of the Grange sewing contest, a Massachusetts man won a Grand Prize for needlework, and an Oregon boy won second prize in the children's section of the stuffed-toy contest. But they were exceptional. Women had their nearly exclusive specialties; men were supposed to concentrate on farm problems.[31]

Some women rejected that division of labor. In 1984, for example, the Chairman of the Women's Activities Committee in the Michigan State Grange represented her sisters at a "Workshop for Women in Agriculture" at which expert women spoke about agricultural financing, marketing, technology, and reform activities. She came away convinced that women should "speak up and take an active part in promoting our business and products." Her only specific suggestions were that Grange women cooperate with American Agri-Women and Women for the Survival of Agriculture in Michigan and that they do something about their appearance. We "need not look like fashion models," she told her sisters, "but we should put our best foot forward and present ourselves as successful business people." Looking "dowdy" was no way to promote agriculture.[32]

Women's activities continued through the 1980s in some familiar ways; service projects, especially a program in aid of deaf people, which the National Grange authorized in 1970, still got a great share of the sisters' energy.[33] But Grange women also departed from their customary activities in two striking ways. First, they withdrew from the contests that had dominated home economics work since the 1950s. In 1987, nine years after the director of women's activities for the Indiana State Grange said that her field consisted "mostly of contests in sewing, crocheting, needlework, and baking," one of her successors reported that Indiana Grange women had produced only half of their quota of garments for the National Grange sewing contest. Then the national women's activities director announced that the great contest's last winners would be recognized at the November 1988 National Grange session. Its decline must surely have been symptomatic of the Order's falling membership; diminishing numbers of women produced diminishing numbers of contest entries.[34] It may also have reflected Grange women's changing interests.

Those changing interests led a few women to new places of leadership in the Order. Joanne Passmore, historian of the Delaware State Grange, became the first woman Secretary of the National Grange in 1985; Jeanne Davies, Master of the Colorado State Grange, became the first woman member of the National Grange Executive Committee in 1986; and Mary Buffington, who directed women's activities for the National Grange starting in 1980, became the first woman National Grange Lecturer in 1987. Davies explains their sudden rise to national leadership as the result of "overall changes in the attitude of the general population," which Grangers adopted without any explicit recognition that they had taken a new direction. She recalls that National Grange members gave "no particular thought" to Passmore's gender in 1985. Rather than consciously choosing to open a new office to women members, they simply elected someone whom they considered dedicated and efficient. Davies also suggests that a recent increase in the number of women state Grange Masters helped to prepare the way for change in the National Grange. She became Master of the Colorado State Grange in 1981; four other women have since held that office in other states.[35]

The women who now help to lead the National Grange resemble prominent sisters of previous generations. Their forerunners were typically high school or normal school graduates; current women leaders are also more than ordinarily educated. Buffington has an A.A. degree, Passmore holds a B.S. in agriculture and an M.A. in agricultural journalism, and Davies studied home economics at Colorado State University, intending to become a teacher, but married before finishing her degree. Also like many of their predecessors, the current leaders participate in a wide range of community and religious activities. Buffington serves on boards that direct public health services and extension work in her county; Passmore is a long-time 4-H leader and has been a trustee of her public library and of the Wilmington Friends School; Davies helped to found her county's library system and has been an officer of several library organizations, clerk of Deer Trail Friends Church, a Sunday and Bible school teacher, and a 4-H leader. None of the three reports professional teaching experience, but they have all been deeply involved in education. And all of them are married to farmers, have raised families, and value traditional domestic crafts. A member of the Master Farm Homemaker Guild, Davies has baked a great many pies for Grange dinners while also helping to lead the Order at its highest levels.[36]

The Order's present women leaders, much more than their predecessors, take vocal parts in Grange efforts to protect rural and agricultural interests. Passmore has advocated farmland preservation, conducted farm conservation tours, and participated in the Delaware Environmental Legacy Symposium. And Davies, as Master of the Colorado State Grange, regularly lobbies her state legislature on matters, such as water policy, that affect farm interests. Legislators and men representing other farm organizations were at first surprised to find a woman at work among them, but she thinks that they have come to accept her. She also addresses farm problems in speeches to the Grange itself. Her 1985 address to the Colorado State Grange was full of gloomy statistics about rising costs of farm operations, falling prices of farm products, and people driven off the land. The facts were all too familiar, but Davies' response to them underlined their human significance. "This will be the last planting season for many," stated a brother, continuing her speech after she left the rostrum in tears.[37]

Earlier Grange women left such hard matters to the men. Now Davies speaks and writes about them in a distinctive voice, full of deeply felt sympathy for her neighbors and friends. She takes a strong interest in home economics and bakes pies, too, but is certainly less confined to women's sphere than her predecessors were. She has achieved a greater degree of "mutuality" than they did, while also continuing women's distinctive, domestic Grange activities. Clearly, the boundary between women's and men's spheres, which Grange women could always cross at some points, is now more permeable than ever.

NOTES

1. *Survey* 55 (1 February 1926): 564.
2. *The Michigan Patron* 15 (April 1937): 10–11.
3. Cott, *The Grounding of Modern Feminism*, 85.
4. "The Story of Myself," a typescript in the Dora Stockman Papers, University Archives and Historical Collection, Michigan State University.
5. Ibid; Dora H. Stockman, *Farmerkin's Farm Rhymes* (Lansing: Henry R. Pattengill Publisher, 1911), Preface, 15.
6. Dora H. Stockman, *Book of Dialogs* (Lansing: Henry R. Pattengill Publisher, 1913), Preface, 1–6, 102–10.
7. *Happy Valley*, a typescript in the Dora Stockman Papers, University Archives and Historical Collections, Michigan State University; Gene Stratton-Porter's *Freckles* (1904) and *A Girl of the Limberlost* (1909) come to mind in this connection.
8. These sections of her dissertation are in Dora Stockman Papers, University Archives and Historical Collection, Michigan State University.
9. Rosters of state officers in National Grange *Proceedings* from 1920 through 1975; see also discussion of women state officers from 1895 through 1920 in Chapter 1 and of Mary Buffington near the end of this epilogue.
10. Gardner, *The Grange*, 205, 214; *Journal of Proceedings of the National Grange of Patrons of Husbandry*, 1926, 129–30.
11. *Journal of Proceedings of the National Grange of Patrons of Husbandry*, 1926, 1927 and 1928, home economics committee reports.
12. *National Grange Monthly* 26 (May 1929): 8.
13. *Boston Sunday Globe* 15 (September 1929).
14. *Pennsylvania Grange News* 23 (April 1926): 4; 24 (July 1927): 6.
15. *Journal of Proceedings of the National Grange of Patrons of Husbandry*, 1929, home economics report.
16. *Journal of Proceedings of the National Grange of Patrons of Husbandry*, 1930, home economics report; *Pennsylvania Grange News* 24 (March 1928): 12.
17. *Journal of Proceedings of the National Grange of Patrons of Husbandry*, 1930, home economics report.

18. *National Grange Monthly* 27 (October 1930): 11; 28 (May 1931): 5.

19. See rosters of state Grange officers in the *Proceedings* for this period.

20. *Journal of Proceedings of the National Grange of Patrons of Husbandry*, 1931, home economics report; *The Grange in Kansas, 1872–1973* (N.p.: Kansas State Grange, n.d.), 68–70.

21. *Journal of Proceedings of the National Grange of Patrons of Husbandry*, 1932 and 1967, home economics reports.

22. *Journal of Proceedings of the National Grange of Patrons of Husbandry*, 1940, 1941, 1942, 1943, 1944, home economics reports.

23. *Journal of Proceedings of the National Grange of Patrons of Husbandry*, 1945, 1947, home economics reports; James H. Madison, "Reformers and the Rural Church, 1900–1950," *Journal of American History* 73 (December 1986): 645–68 discusses outside efforts to diagnose and cure the ills of rural churches. Grangers made broadly similar efforts from inside their communities.

24. *The Maryland Farmer* (March 1954), clipping in the A. B. Hamilton scrapbook, Archives of the Maryland State Grange, Historical Manuscripts and Archives Department, University of Maryland College Park Libraries.

25. *Pennsylvania Grange History: Completing 100 Years of Service 1873–1973* (N.p.: Pennsylvania State Grange, 1973): 21–22.

26. *Journal of Proceedings of the National Grange of Patrons of Husbandry*, 1912, home economics report.

27. *The Grange in Kansas*, 73.

28. *Journal of Proceedings of the National Grange of Patrons of Husbandry*, 1966, home economics report.

29. *California Golden Inspirations* (N.p.: California State Grange, 1960): 9.

30. *The Indianapolis Star* 5 (January 1978).

31. *Journal of Proceedings of the National Grange of Patrons of Husbandry*, 1985, women's activities report.

32. *Michigan Patron* 69 (April 1984): 5.

33. "Grange Deaf Activities," an undated leaflet, and information given orally by Jacqueline Bishop. Originally supervised by the Grange women's activities department, the program of services to the deaf still depends heavily on women's efforts. Beulah Winter, a Michigan Grange leader, has directed the services through most of their history. Participants conduct sign-language classes, contribute to schools for the deaf, befriend children in those schools, warn hearing people of noise hazards, and "bake a LOT of cookies using the Grange 'I Love You' sign cookie cutter." Their activities continue the tradition of service that began with the first women's committees a century ago.

34. *Indianapolis Star* 5 (January 1978); *Journal of Proceedings of the Indiana State Grange*, 1987, 39–42; *National Grange Newsletter* 82 (August–September 1988); Harry Massey, Director of Membership Development for the National Grange, to Marti, 21 May 1990, says that the Order's total membership in the U.S. was 504,742 in 1970; 459,173 in 1975; 417,274 in 1980; 359,443 in 1985; and 323,650 in 1989. Massey sees the Order's condition as a reflection "of the economic viability of rural communities."

35. Jeanne Davies, Denver, to Marti, 26 September 1988.

36. Biographical information provided by the National Grange; Carol Hof-

fecker, ed., *A Legacy from Delaware Women* (Wilmington, Middle Atlantic Press, 1987), 55–56; *The High Plains Journal* 10 (October 1983 and 14 November 1983); *The Colorado Granger* 57 (April 1981): 1.

37. *Rocky Mountain News* 17 (September 1985).

Conclusion

The Grange has always been a family organization; it has always brought men and women together. But it has also encouraged women to co-operate with each other in specific ways, to devote their shares of Grange programs and publications to domestic topics and women's rights, and to form their own committees on woman's work, home economics, and women's activities. Grange women, therefore have pursued "strategies of mutuality" and of "sisterhood" as well.

Grange founders not only included women in the Order but also promised to treat them as fully equal to men. Their practice of equality was limited at first; women cooked and exerted a salutary influence at Grange meetings but did not hold offices or participate in units above the local, or subordinate, level. That changed very quickly. The Grange created the largely ornamental women's offices of Lady Assistant Steward, Ceres, Pomona, and Flora by 1869. And the 1873 revision of the National Grange constitution admitted women to the Order's state and national units, almost always by virtue of their husbands' memberships. At the same time, a scattering of women became local Grange Secretaries, Lecturers, and sometimes even Masters. Their numbers increased around the turn of the century. Sarah Baird was Master of the Minnesota State Grange for seventeen years beginning in 1895; the proportion of state Grange Secretaries and Lecturers who were women rose steeply then, especially in relatively weak Grange states; and a great many women became Secretaries and Lecturers of their local Granges at about the same time. Kenyon Butterfield, a practiced observer of rural institutions including the Grange, guessed in 1901 that a majority of local Grange Lecturers were women, and Jennie Buell's 1921 book about

Grange leadership consistently uses feminine pronouns to describe Lecturers. Buell also suggests that Lecturers, who were responsible for planning Grange programs, had changed from authorities who really lectured to tactful managers of human relations who tried to elicit all of their brothers' and sisters' contributions. Responsibilities changed along with gender; the distinction between men's and women's forms of leadership continued even as women moved into an originally male office and achieved local or regional prominence.

The women who helped to lead their Granges varied in obvious ways. Marie Howland and Sarah Baird had strikingly different ideological complexions, and Jennie Buell's independent career contrasted sharply with Mary Mayo's domesticity. The early Granges attracted a handful of radicals, like Howland; a few career women, like Buell and Dr. Hannah McK. Lyons, helped to lead the early twentieth-century Granges; and conventionally domestic women predominated through the whole period considered here. But the sisters also shared some broad characteristics. Relatively well-educated, typically high school or normal school graduates, they had often taught before marrying. Pedagogical experience, Jennie Buell observed, was just what they needed to be successful Lecturers. Most of them were religious in mainline Protestant or unconventional ways, and they were all dedicated to the moral improvement of their communities. Finally, the sisters who left records of their thought shared a deep concern about farm women who worked too hard, had too few social and intellectual opportunities, and, consequently, fell short of their best possibilities. Almost all of them agreed that those best possibilities were domestic. The "cult of true womanhood" had grown up among townsfolk and poorly matched rural conditions, but Grange women embraced it nonetheless.

Grangers said that farm women needed to overcome drudgery before they could meet the highest standards of domesticity. Mindless, repetitive, ceaseless labor stultified women and often, Grangers said with scant evidence but obvious conviction, drove them mad. Drudgery was to be overcome by demanding more consideration from men, but even more by women's rational examination of their tasks. They had to find ways of working more efficiently; Grange women published a mass of household hints in aid of that. And women had to distinguish between essential responsibilities and time-consuming busywork. Serve fresh apples instead of pie, Mary Mayo taught. Be guided by the scientific authority of home economics, a chorus of sisters urged. When college home economics departments proliferated early in this century, Grange women transmitted their lessons through the Order's programs, publications, and committees. Home economics committees, begun in 1910, were their principal network for diffusing scientific wisdom. Home economics is controversial now; historians accuse its founders of denigrating women's craft traditions and promoting the urban separation of men's and women's spheres among rural people. But Grange women thought that it was the sovereign cure for drudgery.

Grange women also demanded acknowledgment of the civic responsibilities that accompanied domesticity. Informed by Frances Willard's doctrine of "home protection" and by John Ruskin's very similar teaching that "woman has a personal work and duty relating to her home, and a public work and duty which is also the expansion of that," Grangers argued that women needed votes to defend their domestic sanctuaries against social evils, especially alcohol. In Aileen Kraditor's very pertinent terms, Grangers emphasized the argument from expediency that superceded the argument from natural right with which nineteenth-century equal suffrage advocacy began. The Order's most committed suffragists, notably Elizabeth Gifford, also continued the argument from natural rights as a secondary theme. Further, they argued that the Order's many professions of respect for women, especially in its 1874 Declaration of Purposes, required it to support equal suffrage. That last argument forced suffragists to overlook early Grangers' many assurances that they did not favor women's rights in any political sense. Grange suffrage advocates did that artfully enough to persuade the Order, finally, that it had always favored equal suffrage as a clear implication of its first principles.

The nineteenth amendment, ratified in 1920, ended the long campaign for equal suffrage. No later public issue ever took its place for Grange women. But the years after 1920 resembled the Order's first half-century more than they differed from it. Women's freedom to participate in politics did not mean that they abandoned their old tradition of acting on public matters through private, voluntary organizations. Women still used the Grange for public purposes, to denounce cigarettes, promote patriotism, contribute to war efforts, strengthen rural churches, and beautify their communities. No one or closely related cluster of those causes absorbed their energies as suffrage and prohibition had done, but their tradition of voluntary action remained vital.

Their commitment to domesticity persisted, too. Rural life, as they echoed Theodore Roosevelt, was the foundation of American civilization; the foundation would crack, they feared, unless rural homes were attractive enough to hold young people on the land. That was all perfectly familiar. But their domestic rhetoric and activities changed in three striking ways. First, they said much less about drudgery after the 1920s than they had before. Second, Grange women devoted an enormous share of their energies to contests of various kinds, especially after the Order's craft competitions began to attract generous commercial sponsors in the 1950s. And, finally, because those contests got so much of women's attention and energy, Grange domesticity was more narrowly focused on household crafts from the 1950s to the 1980s than it had ever been before. The old Grange combination of specialized women's activities and "mutuality" between men and women is hard to discern in the records of those years, as are the political aspirations that a broad understanding of domesticity had inspired among earlier sisters.

In the 1980s some women asked their sisters to "speak up" for agriculture rather than contenting themselves with purely domestic interests. Then a few women began to take positions of leadership that gave them authority to speak about farm problems. They did that without abandoning Grange women's traditional domesticity; they did women's work and men's as well. Continuing, or reviving, the old combination of "mutuality" and "sisterhood," they enlarged the Order's practice of its equalitarian principle just as Marie Howland, Sarah Baird, and many others had done before. The Grange has always stood for equality, to be sure, but its implementation has repeatedly grown since Aaron Grosh assured conservatives that the sisters were "Not there politically."

Note on Sources

The historical bibliography on rural women is relatively short. Historians of women, like their colleagues who study other aspects of the past, generally prefer urban subjects and settings. Most of the exceptions find pioneers more interesting than the settled farmers and other rural people who have predominated in the Grange. Consequently, only a handful of studies are very directly concerned with the subject considered here.

Douglas Charles Hebb, "The Woman Movement in the California State Grange, 1873–1880" (M.A. thesis, University of California, 1950) is most directly related to this study. Hebb's frequent citation here testifies to his work's helpfulness. Other directly informative studies include Warren Gates, "Her Voices at the Picnic: Women's Programs at Williams Grove, The 1890s," a paper presented to the Zatae Logsdorff Conference in Women's Studies in 1978; Vanette M. Schwartz, "The Role of Rural Women in Midwestern Farm Organizations, 1870–1900," a paper presented to the "Female Sphere Conference" at New Harmony in 1981; Mary Jo Wagner, "Farms, Families, and Reform: Women in the Farmers' Alliance and Populist Party" (Ph.D. diss., University of Oregon, 1986); and Julie Roy Jeffrey, "Women in the Southern Farmers' Alliance," *Feminist Studies* 3 (Fall 1975): 72–91. Gates' essay is informative about Grange women's rhetoric in a particular setting; Schwartz makes explicit comparisons between the roles that Grange and Alliance women played in their organizations; Wagner and Jeffrey focus on Alliance women, but their studies suggest comparisons between their subjects and Grange women.

A few recent studies of rural women have informed this essay in important, if general, ways. Nancy Grey Osterud, "Strategies of Mutuality: Relations Among Women and Men in an Agricultural Community" (Ph.D. diss., Brown University, 1984) and " 'She Helped Me Hay It as Good as a Man': Relations Among Women and Men in an Agricultural Community" in Carol Groneman and Mary Beth Norton, *"To Toil the Livelong Day": America's Women at Work, 1780–1980* (Ithaca: Cornell University Press, 1987) have been particularly suggestive. So have Mary Neth, "Preserving the family farm: Farm families and communities in the Midwest, 1900–1940" (Ph.D. diss., University of Wisconsin, 1987) and "Building the Base: Farm Women, The Rural Community, and Farm Organizations in the Midwest, 1900–1940" in Wava G. Haney and Jane B. Knowles, *Women and Farming: Changing Roles, Changing Structures* (Boulder: Westview Press, 1988), and Deborah Fink, *Open Country Iowa: Rural Women, Tradition and Change* (Albany: State University of New York Press, 1986.) Osterud, Neth, and Fink all suggest ways of thinking about two standard themes in women's history, the ideology of separate spheres and sisterhood, in rural settings. The most widely cited studies in which those themes were developed, notably Carroll Smith-Rosenberg, "The Female World of Love and Ritual: Relations Between Women in Nineteenth Century America," *Signs* 1 (Autumn 1975): 1–29 and Barbara Leslie Epstein, *The Politics of Domesticity: Women, Evangelism and Temperance in Nineteenth Century America* (Middletown: Wesleyan University Press, 1981), deal with town women. Osterud, Neth, and Fink consider the tension between townsfolks' ideology of gender, which commanded deference in the countryside, and the relations of "mutuality," the sharing of work and social enjoyments among women and men, that characterized rural life.

Helpful studies of women's organizations include: Ruth Bordin, *Women and Temperance: The Quest for Power and Liberty, 1873–1900* (Philadelphia: Temple University Press, 1981); Karen J. Blair, *The Clubwoman as Feminist: True Womanhood Redefined, 1868–1914* (New York: Holmes and Meier Publishers, Inc., 1980); and Theodora Penny Martin, *The Sound of Our Own Voices: Women's Study Clubs, 1860–1910* (Boston: Beacon Press, 1987). Bordin provides an authoritative guide to the WCTU, which many Grange women joined or simply admired, while Blair and Martin consider the women's clubs that resembled the Grange in general ways and shared some leadership with it.

The books that most directly informed this study's treatment of the woman movement and of the equal suffrage cause in particular are: Nancy M. Cott, *The Grounding of Modern Feminism* (New Haven: Yale University Press, 1987) and Aileen Kraditor, *The Ideas of the Woman Suffrage Movement, 1890–1920* (New York: W. W. Norton, 1981). Cott's book distinguishes between the nineteenth-century woman movement and twentieth-century feminism and describes the nineteenth amendment's impact on reform-minded women. Kraditor's book illuminates the intellectual history of suffrage advocacy, as Cott's also does.

Home economics, a major interest among Grange women, has inspired a small body of scholarship that informs several parts of this study. Glenna Matthews, *"Just a Housewife": The Rise and Fall of Domesticity in America* (New York: Oxford University Press, 1987) is an elegant, critical study of the subject; Barbara Miller Solomon, *In the Company of Educated Women: A History of Women and Higher Education in America* (New Haven: Yale University Press, 1985) includes brief references to home economics and particularly to women educators' ambivalence about it. Also helpful are: Linda Fritschner, "The Rise and Fall of Home Economics" (Ph.D. diss. University of California–Davis, 1973); Isabel Bevier, *Home Economics in Education* (Philadelphia: J. B. Lippincott Company, 1924); Mabel Newcomer, *A Century of Higher Education for American Women* (New York: Harper and Brothers Publishers, 1959); and Maude Gilchrist, *The First Three Decades of Home Economics at Michigan State College, 1896–1926* (East Lansing: Michigan State College, 1947).

Historical writing about the Grange includes Solon Buck, *The Granger Movement* (Cambridge: Harvard University Press, 1933), which has little to say about the Order's women and their interests. Dennis Sven Nordin, *Rich Harvest: A History of the Grange, 1867–1900* (Jackson: University Press of Mississippi, 1974) is more useful for the present purpose. It describes activities and subjects that interested Grange women and provides an exhaustive bibliography. Thomas A. Woods, *Knights of the Plow: Oliver H. Kelley and the Origins of the Grange in Republican Ideology* (Ames: Iowa State University Press, 1991) brings the early Grange into the increasingly wide-ranging historical conversation about republicanism and, in doing so, puts Oliver Kelley in a new and intriguing light. Unlike many other historians of the Grange, Woods understands that Grangers did not immediately embrace women's rights; they first saw women, he suggests, as "Republican Mothers" whose vital civic responsibilities were to be discharged at home. Charles M. Gardner, *The Grange–Friend of the Farmer* (Washington: National Grange, 1949) is a richly detailed insider's view of the organization. Gardner was a Grange leader nationally and in Massachusetts for many years before he wrote his book. Other insiders' histories are: Oliver Hudson Kelley, *Origin and Progress of the Order of the Patrons of Husbandry in the United States: A History from 1866 to 1873* (Philadelphia: J. A. Wagenseller, 1875), which is valuable for the correspondence between Kelley and other founders it reproduces; D. Wyatt Aiken, *The Grange, Its Origin, Progress and Educational Purposes* (Washington: National Grange, 1883), which is an early southern leader's account of the Order's first years; and Thomas Clark Atkeson, *Semi-Centennial History of the Patrons of Husbandry* (New York: Orange Judd, 1926), which is a thoughtful account by one of the Order's outstanding leaders. Other studies of national Grange history are: Fritiof Ander, "The Immigrant Church and the Patrons of Husbandry," *Agricultural History* 8 (October 1934): 155–68; William D. Barns, "Oliver Hudson Kelley and the Genesis of the Grange: A Reappraisal," *Agricultural History* 41 (July 1967): 229–42; Sister M. Thomas More Bertels, O.S.F., "The National Grange: Progressives on the Land" (Ph.D. diss., Catholic University of America, 1962); and Sarah Margaret Stephenson, "The Social and Educational Aspects of the Grange, 1870–1934" (M.S. thesis, University of Wisconsin, 1935), which is particularly informative about women's participation in the Order. Another study of that last topic is Donald B. Marti, "Sisters of the Grange: Rural Feminism in the Late Nineteenth Century," *Agricultural History* 58 (July 1984): 247–61. [The use of "feminism" in that title is anachronistic; see Nancy F. Cott, *The Grounding of Modern Feminism* (New Haven: Yale University Press, 1987.)]

Historians and Grangers themselves have also written about the Order in particular states, regions, and localities. Studies that have been helpful here are: Leonard Allen, *History of the New York State Grange* (Watertown: New York State Grange, 1934); William D. Barns, *The West Virginia State Grange: The First Century, 1873–1973* (Morgantown: Morgantown Printing and Binding Co., 1973); Fred Brenckman, *History of the Pennsylvania State Grange* (Harrisburg: Pennsylvania State Grange, 1949); Robert Arnold Calvert, "The Southern Grange: The Farmer's Search for Identity in the Gilded Age" (Ph.D. diss., University of Texas, 1969); Sue S. Carpenter, "History of Centre Grange From 1874 to 1949" in *History of Centre Grange No. 11 Patrons of Husbandry 1874–1974* (Centreville, Delaware: Centre Grange No. 11, 1974); *The Connecticut Grangers* (New Haven: Industrial Publishing Co., 1900); Harriet Ann Crawford, *The Washington State Grange: A Romance of Democracy* (Portland: Binfords and Mort, Publishers, 1940); James S. Ferguson, "The Granger Movement in Mississippi" (M.A. thesis, Louisiana State University, 1940); Wayne E. Fuller, "A History of the Grange in Colorado" (M.A. thesis, University of Denver, 1949); Samuel Carleton Guptill, "The Grange in Maine from 1874–1940" (Ph.D. diss., University of Maine, 1973); Arba L. Henry, "An Analysis of the Pennsylvania State Grange" (Ed.D. thesis, Pennsylvania State University, 1984); Janet Hopkins, *History of the Rhode Island State Grange* (N.p.: Rhode Island State Grange, 1939); Guy B. Horton, *A History of the Grange in Vermont* (Montpelier: Vermont State Grange, 1926); Mary and Eben Jenkins, *Maryland State Grange: The First Hundred Years* (N.p.: State Grange, 1974); *The Grange in Kansas 1872–1973* (N.p.: Kansas State Grange, n.d.); LaVerne Marquart, *Wisconsin's Agricultural Heritage: The Grange, 1871–1971* (Lake Mills: Rural Life Publishing Co., 1972); Donald B. Marti, "Woman's Work in the Grange: Mary Ann Mayo of Michigan, 1882–1903," *Agricultural History* 56 (April 1982): 439–52; Joanne Passmore, *History of the Delaware State Grange* (N.p.: Delaware State Grange,

1975); Rexford Booth Sherman, "The Grange in Maine and New Hampshire" (Ph.D. diss., Boston University, 1973); Ralph W. Smith, *History of the Iowa State Grange* (Manchester: Iowa State Grange, 1946); Ralph W. Smith, *Newton No. 1* (Newton: Iowa State Grange, 1967); Mildred Throne, "The Grange in Iowa, 1868–1875," *Iowa Journal of History* 47 (October 1949): 289–324; and Fred Trump, *The Grange in Michigan: An Agricultural History of Michigan Over the Past Ninety Years* (Grand Rapids: The Author, 1963).

No single repository holds a definitive collection of Grange papers. Indeed, many important papers have not been collected at all. C. Jerome Davis, a Grange leader and historian in Indiana, discovered in the course of his research that most records of the Indiana State Grange had been destroyed by someone who considered old materials useless. The same misfortune occurred in Iowa. Ralph W. Smith, *Newton No. 1* (Newton: Iowa State Grange, 1967), 6 reports that the "Iowa State Grange, in the early 1900s, destroyed all old records and material, saving only the original bond given by Montgomery Ward to the State Grange and the Secretary's dues received book." But some papers survive. The National Grange Records at the Cornell University Library were useful here mainly for a few letters that Marie Howland wrote to William Saunders; Cornell also holds the New York State Grange Records, which include many local Grange minute books. The Division of Archives and Manuscripts at the Minnesota Historical Society holds some state Grange records, Sarah Baird's diaries, and minutes of Minnehaha Grange No. 398; Paul Hesterman, "The History of Edina," a typescript in the Minneapolis Public Library, puts the Minnehaha Grange in the context of its community's history. The Special Collections Department of the University of Maryland College Park Libraries has the Archives of the Maryland State Grange, which are a diverse body of manuscripts and clippings, some of them illustrative of women's activities. The Huntington Library has the Jeanne C. Carr papers, and the National City, California, Public Library has Flora Kimball's scrapbooks. Robert S. Mayo provided copies of his notes about his grandmother, Mary Mayo; the University Archives and Historical Collection at Michigan State University holds the Mary Mayo letters, a few other documents by and about Mayo, and the Dora Stockman Papers. The minutes of Olive Grange No. 189 at the Indiana Historical Society document Grange meetings in which women played little role and caution against excessively sweeping generalizations about the Order's receptiveness to women's contributions. The Cyrus H. Jasperce Papers and the Barber Buell Papers in the Michigan Historical Collection at the University of Michigan's Bentley Library are informative about some women leaders, especially Jennie Buell. The Eliza Gifford manuscripts at the Patterson Library and Art Gallery, in Westfield, New York illustrate Grange women's rights advocacy. And a typescript on

"Minnie and Cyrus Fenwick, Pioneer Ministers of Burns," in the Wyoming State Historical Research and Publication Division," provides information on an exceptional Grange woman.

The most valuable sources for this study were Grange journals, weekly and monthly publications that reported the Order's news and printed its speeches, essays, poems, and other literature. As Dennis Sven Nordin's bibliography shows, many publications served at least briefly as Grange organs. Journals that contributed to this study are: *American Grange Bulletin and Scientific Farmer* for the entire Order from 1896 through 1905; *Dirigo Rural* for Maine and New England more generally in the 1870s; the *Farmer's Friend and Grange Advocate* for Pennsylvania from 1891 through 1912; the *Grange Visitor* for Michigan in the last quarter of the nineteenth century; the *Hennepin County Mirror* for Minnesota in 1882 and 1883; the *Husbandman* for New York in the last quarter of the nineteenth century; the *Indiana Farmer* for the late 1870s and early 1880s; the *Michigan Patron* for the early twentieth century; the *Minnesota Monthly* for 1869; *National Grange* and *National Grange Monthly* for the entire Order from 1907 through 1951; the *Pacific Rural Press* for the west, especially California, in the early 1880s; *Pennsylvania Grange News* for the years from 1905 through 1933; and the Wisconsin State Grange *Bulletin* for the decade beginning in 1874.

Some journals are more useful than others for the study of Grange women. *The Farmer's Friend and Grange Advocate*, the *Grange Visitor*, the *Husbandman, National Grange*, and *National Grange Monthly*, and the Wisconsin State Grange *Bulletin* contain an abundance of women's writing. Apart from the differing amounts of such material that they attracted, or for which they made room, the journals were very much alike. The women who wrote for them had a few themes, which are described mainly in the third through sixth chapters of this study, and addressed them in similar ways in every region and through the whole period of this study. Women's contributions to the journals were remarkably homogeneous.

Grangers have also published books, pamphlets, and articles in general magazines. The books prominently include the Reverend Aaron B. Grosh, *Mentor in the Granges and Homes of Patrons of Husbandry* (New York: Clark and Maynard, 1876). A Universalist minister who confessed that he knew a great deal more about farm houses than he did about barns and fields, Grosh was a perfect example of the liberal clergymen whom Ann Douglas describes in *The Feminization of American Culture* (New York: Knopf, 1977). Such ministers, Douglas argues, were allied with women in pursuit of an "influence" that compensated for the power that both were denied. Grosh emphasized women's importance to the Grange in terms that echoed down through the entire period of this study. A later book of comparable importance is Jennie Buell, *One Wom-*

an's Work for Farm Women (Boston: Whitcomb and Barrows, 1908), which is a Michigan Grange leader's tribute to Mary Mayo, her friend and predecessor. Buell also wrote *The Grange Master and the Grange Lecturer* (New York: Harcourt Brace and Company, 1921). By the time Buell published that book, most Lecturers were women; her description of the office is also a description of women's most important role in the Order. Ezra Carr, *The Patrons of Husbandry on the Pacific Coast* (San Francisco, 1875) contains a chapter on "The Industrial Education of Women," which summarizes some of the Order's most characteristic educational ideas. Less important, but illustrative of attitudes that have been pervasive in the Grange, are Dora Stockman's children's books, *Farmerkin's Farm Rhymes* (Lansing: Henry R. Pattengill, 1913) and *Book of Dialogs* (Lansing: Henry R. Pattengill, 1913).

Grangers have published an enormous quantity of pamphlets. In the 1870s, for example, the National Grange reprinted a few of its leaders' speeches as the Bryan Fund Publications. Some of those undated, ephemeral leaflets are discussed near the beginning of Chapter 6 because they illustrate early, conservative Grange attitudes toward women's rights and, particularly, equal suffrage. They are available on microfiche at the State Historical Society of Wisconsin. Later, probably in the 1880s, the National Grange Lecturer's office issued a series of leaflets that took a far more positive view of the Order's tendency to encourage women's public interests. Flora Kimball's *Woman's Relationship to Society Through the Grange* is a particularly interesting example. The leaflets have been collected at the National Agricultural Library. Other valuable pamphlets include: Mortimer Whitehead, ed., *A Silver Jubilee: Twenty-Fifth Anniversary of the First Farmer's Grange in the World* (Washington: National Grange, 1893); *The Grange. What It Has Accomplished. What It Is Still Laboring to Accomplish. Declaration of Purposes. Who are Eligible to Membership. And How to Organize a Subordinate Grange* (Mechanicsburg: Farmer's Friend, 189 [?]); and L. J. Taber, *Lecturer's Handbook* (N.p.: Ohio State Grange, 1913).

Grangers occasionally wrote about the Order in general magazines. Kenyon Butterfield, who edited the Michigan *Grange Visitor*, later headed three agricultural colleges, and helped to lead the Country Life Movement, emphasized women's leadership, especially as Lecturers, in "The Grange," *The Forum* (April 1901): 231–42, and their charitable activities in "Recent Grange Work in Michigan," *Outlook* 60 (17 September 1898): 176–79. "What the Grange Has Meant to Me," *The Country Gentleman* 82 (1 December 1917): 36–38, purports to be a young woman's account of the Order's transforming influence on her life; and Marie Howland, "The Patrons of Husbandry," *Lippincott's Magazine of Popular Literature and Science* 12 (September 1873): 338–42, explains the hopes that a particularly radical Granger briefly placed in the Order.

The study also draws upon official Grange documents, including its first constitution, written in 1868, and some later revisions; *Manual and Monitor of Subordinate Granges, of Patrons of Husbandry* (St. Paul: National Grange, 1869); and *Dedication of Grange Halls Adopted By The National Grange at the Ninth Annual Session* (Louisville: National Grange, 1875). The State Historical Society of Wisconsin has many such documents on microfiche. It also has an extensive collection of *Proceedings* for the National Grange and many of its state affiliates. Rosters of subordinate and Pomona Granges published by state Granges were also valuable for identifying the offices in which women were most likely to serve at various times. The Pennsylvania State Grange made its *Register of State, Pomona, and Subordinate Grange Officers* (Mechanicsburg: Farmer's Friend, various dates) available in its Harrisburg office along with other materials.

The kind Pennsylvanians and other present-day Grangers were themselves a source for this study. The acknowledgments at the beginning of this book recognize some especially helpful individuals.

Index

About the Author

DONALD B. MARTI is an Associate Professor of History at Indiana University at South Bend. He has authored numerous articles on agricultural history, as well as the book *Historical Directory of American Agricultural Fairs* (Greenwood, 1986).